LEVEL

XI

3RD EDITION

VOCABULARY
FROM
LATIN AND GREEK ROOTS

A STUDY OF WORD FAMILIES

By: Elizabeth Osborne

Edited by Paul Moliken

Illustrated by Larry Knox

Prestwick House wishes to extend its gratitude to the many contributors whose assistance, comments, and expertise were essential in completing this book.

Prestwick House

P.O. Box 658 • Clayton, DE 19938

1.800.932.4593 • www.prestwickhouse.com

ISBN: 978-1-58049-207-2

3rd Edition 2017

INTRODUCTION

Prestwick House developed *Vocabulary from Latin and Greek Roots* in response to numerous requests for a solid etymology-based vocabulary program. Because the aim of the program is to increase retention of new words as well as to expand students' vocabulary, we chose to organize the Units by meaning rather than alphabetically. A student who associates a root with an idea will be more likely to correctly assess the definition of that root's English derivative.

Each Unit contains at least three Latin and/or Greek roots; one or more English vocabulary words are provided for each root. Unit Thirteen of this book, for example, includes five roots having to do with fire, burning, and flashing. When a student reads through the Unit, he or she will see the key letters that signal the presence of the root in an English word. The letters in the first root of Unit Thirteen form the stems CEND, CENS. Beneath the key letters is the root word from which the English is derived: CENDERE, CENSUM. Students will notice that there are sometimes two forms of the root, and sometimes one. The inclusion of two forms indicates a Latin verb from which English has taken two different forms. CENDERE, for instance, gives us *incendiary*, meaning "inflaming; provoking heat or anger," while CENSUM gives us *incense*, meaning "to infuriate; to make passionately angry." When a root comes from a Latin adjective or noun, only one form will generally be included. Greek roots also appear in only one form.

Beneath the definition of the root, the student will find the word, its pronunciation, part of speech, and English definition. In cases in which an English word has multiple meanings, we have chosen to include only the meaning appropriate to the grade level for which the book is intended. The word *elaborate* in this book, then, is a verb meaning "to explain in greater detail" rather than an adjective meaning "marked by complexity or great detail"; in Level IX, *pedestrian* means "lacking excitement; ordinary and dull," rather than "a traveler on foot." In some instances, students may find it useful to review meanings that do not appear and discuss how they are related to the meaning presented.

If the word has a prefix, or if it is especially difficult to reconcile with its root, the entry will contain an analysis of the parts of the word, followed by a literal definition. *Repulsion* in Level IX, Unit Five, is explained as *re*, meaning "back" + *pulsum*; the literal meaning is "a pushing back."

Finally, each entry provides a sentence using the word and, when appropriate, introduces pertinent synonyms and/or antonyms. For added visual reinforcement of this understanding, mnemonic cartoons appear in each Unit.

Six different kinds of exercise follow the Unit entries. They include three kinds of practice using words in context, one test of a student's ability to infer information based on a word's meaning, one reading comprehension exercise, and one activity in which a student must deduce the meaning of an unfamiliar word based on knowledge of the word's root. By the end of the exercises in each Unit, students will have had thorough practice using the word in context and will be prepared to make the word part of their working vocabulary.

Note: We have changed the form of some vocabulary words to make the sentences and exercises more interesting, eliminate awkward phrasing, and avoid excessive repetition. For example, a noun (*marvel*) may be changed to an adjective (*marvelous*) or a verb (*marveled*).

PREFIXES

A (L.) away from

A (G.) not, no

AB (L.) away from

AD (L.) toward

ALTER (L.) another

AMPHI (G.) around, both

ANA (G.) up

ANTE (L.) before

ANTI (G.) against

CIRCUM (L.) around

CO (L.) with, together

CON (L.) with, together *

CONTRA (L.) against

DE (L.) down, down from

DIA (G.) through

DIS (L.) apart, away from

DYS (G.) bad

E (L.) out of

EC (G.) outside

EM (G.) in, within

EN (G.) in, within

EPI (G.) upon

EX (L.) out of, away from *

HYPER (G.) over

IN (L.) in, into, on, against, not *

INTRO (L.) inside

OB (L.) against

OMNI (L.) every, all

PER (L.) through

PERI (G.) around

POST (L.) after

PRE (L.) before

RE (L.) back, again *

RETRO (L.) backwards

SUB (L.) beneath

SUPER, SUR (L.) above

SYM (G.) with, together

SYN (G.) with, together

TRANS (L.) across

TELE (G.) distant

* Note: *con*, *ex*, *in*, and *re* sometimes serve as *intensifiers*. In such cases, these prefixes simply mean "very."

PRONUNCIATION GUIDE

a = track

ā = mate

ä = father

â = care

e = pet

ē = be

i = bit

ī = bite

o = job

ō = wrote

ô = port

ōō = proof

u = pun

ū = you

û = purr

ə = about, system, supper, circus

WORD LIST FOR LEVEL XI

UNIT 1
belabor
discomfit
edification
elaborate
feasible
laborious
lethargy
liturgy
magnum opus
malfeasance
modus operandi
opulent
surfeit
synergy

UNIT 2
apropos
depose
ecstasy
entity
essence
extant
quintessential
restive
stanch
stasis
static
staunch

UNIT 3
appall
candid
candor
denigrate
incandescent
livid
pallid
pallor
verdant
verdure
viridity

UNIT 4
impair
impeccable
malaise
malign
malinger
negate
negligent
negligible
peccadillo
peccant
pejorative

UNIT 5
bacchanal
bacchic
elegiac
elegy
festoon
fete
jocose
jocular
plaint
plaintive

UNIT 6
acquiesce
languid
languish
languor
quittance
requiem
somnolent
sopor
soporific
vigilant
vigilante

UNIT 7
auspices
auspicious
consort
consortium
destine
fortuitous
fortuity
predestination
propitiate
propitious

UNIT 8
conferment
congested
euphoria
gestate
gesticulate
importunate
importune
insufferable
periphery
preferential
rapport

UNIT 9
desolate
divulge
hoi polloi
monosyllabic
monotone
monotonous
polyglot
polymath
soliloquy
solipsism
vulgar

UNIT 10
catholic
consummate
holistic
parcel
parse
repartee
summation
totalitarian
totality
trenchant
truncate

UNIT 11
annex
ascertain
assertion
certitude
disconcert
dissertation
exertion
liaison
ligature
nexus
obligatory

UNIT 12
accede
adventitious
ambiance
antecedent
circuitous
contravene
parvenu
precedent
sedition
transitory

UNIT 13
conflagration
flagrant
flamboyant
fulminate
illustrative
illustrious
incendiary
incense
inflammatory
luster
refulgent

UNIT 14
abominable
abomination
demonstrative
metaphrase
ominous
paradigm
paraphrase
phraseology
remonstrate
semantic
semiotic

UNIT 15
attrition
contrite
detrimental
detritus
lenient
lenitive
mollify
rudiment
rudimentary
trite

UNIT 16
acclivity
contort
converge
declivity
distort
diverge
implicit
inexplicable
insinuate
proclivity
sinuous

UNIT 17
append
desultory
expendable
exultant
impending
interject
inundate
redound
resilient
subjective
undulate

UNIT 18
deracinate
disseminate
eradicate
florid
flourish
germane
germinal
germinate
irradicable
seminal

UNIT 19
adorn
decorous
decorum
formality
formulaic
formulate
inordinate
ordain
ornate
preordained
suborn

UNIT 20
appraise
appreciable
communal
demerit
excommunicate
incommunicado
meretricious
meritorious
munificent
remunerate

UNIT 21
ablution
alluvial
distill
fluctuate
fluent
instill
lachrymal
lachrymose
lavish
meander
riparian

UNIT 22
cavernous
concave
crevasse
crevice
excavate
fission
fissure
hiatus
orifice
orotund

UNIT ONE

FAC
Latin FACERE, FACTUM, "to make; to do"

DISCOMFIT   (dis kəm´ fit)   v.   to embarrass and confuse
Although the presence of a large audience *discomfited* the violinist, she gave a magnificent performance.
syn: perturb

EDIFICATION   (ed ə fi kā´ shən)   n.   an improvement or enlightenment
L. *aedis*, "building" + *factum = to make a building; to build up*
Mrs. Marple, an etiquette expert, often gives hints for the *edification* of her audience.
syn: betterment

MALFEASANCE   (mal fēz´ əns)   n.   misconduct or wrongdoing, especially by a
            public official
L. *mal*, "bad" + *facere = doing bad*
The reporter uncovered a complex conspiracy intended to hide the mayor's latest *malfeasance*.
syn: impropriety

FEASIBLE   (fēz´ ə bəl)   adj.   capable of being accomplished
The Board of Education could not find a *feasible* solution to the overcrowding of city schools.
syn: possible, achievable   ant: unattainable

SURFEIT   (sûr´ fət)   n.   the condition of being too full; an overabundance
L. *sur*, "over" + *facere = too much made*
A *surfeit* of weapons led to a lack of space in the army's warehouse.
syn: glut, profusion   ant: shortage, dearth

The shark feasted on a SURFEIT of SURFERS.

OPUS
Latin OPUS, OPERIS, "work"
Latin OPS, OPIS, "wealth; power; resource"

MAGNUM OPUS   (mag´ nəm ō´ pəs)   n.   the
            greatest work of an artist, writer, or composer
L. *magnum*, "great" + *opus = great work*
Wagner's "Ring Trilogy" is considered by many to be the composer's *magnum opus*.
syn: pinnacle

▥ *A comfit, like a confection, is a kind of dessert. The word comes from the Latin* confectum, *meaning "that which is prepared"* (L. con, *"together"* + factum = to make *together; to prepare). To* discomfit *originally meant "to ruin someone's preparations or plans" and now simply means "to embarrass."*

▥ *Both* feasible *and* malfeasance *are derived from the French* faisant, *"doing," which, in turn, comes from* facere.

MODUS OPERANDI (mō dəs   ä pə rän´ dī) *n.* a specific manner of working
L. *modus*, "way" + *operandi*, "of working" = *a way of working*
The criminal's *modus operandi* was one that the police had seen only rarely in the past.
syn: method

OPULENT (o´ pū lənt) *adj.* possessing or exhibiting great wealth; affluent
Having made his fortune in computer sales, Kit retired to an *opulent* estate on a private island.

ERG
Greek ERGON, "work"

SYNERGY (si´ nər jē) *n.* the power that results from the combination of two
        or more forces
G. *syn*, "together" + *ergon* = *working together*
The *synergy* of the two networks allowed for faster and more powerful transmission of information.
syn: confluence

LITURGY (li´ tər jē) *n.* a pattern of prayer or worship
G. *leiton*, "town gathering" + *ergon* = *public work*
In a traditional Roman Catholic Mass, the priest leads the congregation in the *liturgy*.

LETHARGY (lə´ thər jē) *n.* a state of sluggishness, inactivity, and apathy
G. *lethe*, "forgetfulness" + *a*, "without" + *ergon* = *forgetful idleness*
As Jack's *lethargy* increased, he found himself unable to concentrate on his work.
syn: laziness   *ant: activity*

LABOR
Latin LABOR, "work"

LABORIOUS (lə bôr´ ē əs) *adj.* requiring mental or physical effort
Reading the article was so *laborious* that I left the library exhausted.
syn: tiresome   *ant: effortless*

BELABOR (bē lā´ bər) *v.* 1. to discuss in too much detail
                              2. to attack
1. There is no need to *belabor* this topic; let's talk about something else.
2. Movie critics *belabored* that actor for his terrible movies.

ELABORATE (ē la´ bər āt) *v.* to explain in greater detail
L. *e*, "out of" + *labor* = *to work out*
When asked to *elaborate* on his proposal for the new park, the mayor said only that it was in the planning stages.

The bosom of America is open to receive not only the Opulent & respectable Stranger, but the oppressed & persecuted of all Nations & Religions; whom we shall wellcome to a participation of all our rights & previleges.
—George Washington

In Greek, a leitourgia was a public service, the sort that might be performed at a community gathering. Liturgy now means a service performed at a religious gathering or service.

EXERCISES - UNIT ONE

Exercise I. Complete the sentence in a way that shows you understand the meaning of the italicized vocabulary word.

1.   When they reached the *opulent* port city, the sailors saw…

2.   Because their work could only be accomplished through many *laborious* tasks, the farmhands…

3.   For the *edification* of her students, the sculpting teacher explained that…

4.   George was *discomfited* by his parents' shouting match because…

5.   The amazing *synergy* of the two companies became evident when…

6.   Gerald would not *elaborate* on his plan to leave town because…

7.   When the architect finished her *magnum opus*, she felt…

8.   Executives may be involved in corporate *malfeasance* when they…

9.   Donna felt that William was *belaboring* the point when he…

10. The farmer's plan to irrigate his crops twice a week was *feasible* because…

11. Parents can eliminate *lethargy* in younger children by…

12. The train robbers' *modus operandi* involved…

13. The *liturgy* at the cathedral usually started with…

14. Because they had a *surfeit* of qualified applicants for the position, company managers…

Exercise II. Fill in the blank with the best word from the choices below. One word will not be used.

modus operandi   laborious   feasible   edification   discomfit

1.   Liz found organizing her closet such a(n) _____ task that she decided she would never do it again.

2.   The surgeon's _____ changed along with the advances in technology.

3.   The magician revealed some of his secrets for the _____ of his audience.

4.   Fearing that his large, rowdy St. Bernard would _____ his dinner guests, Carl put the dog in its outdoor pen.

Fill in the blank with the best word from the choices below. One word will not be used.

lethargy   belabor   feasible   liturgy   elaborate   surfeit

5. Although many of her past schemes had not been _____, this time Rosa's invention seemed sure to work.

6. A printout of the _____ was available for newcomers unfamiliar with the religious service.

7. Bill attributed his recent _____ to the rainy weather and lack of excitement at his job.

8. When the quiz-show contestant began to _____ an issue related to his missed question, the host cut to a commercial.

9. Noticing the _____ of stray kittens at the shelter, Maureen offered to take some home.

Fill in the blank with the best word from the choices below. One word will not be used.

magnum opus   malfeasance   lethargy   synergy   elaborate   opulent

10. The acting coach hoped to develop some sort of _____ among the members of his ensemble.

11. Although Scott hinted that something major would be taking place in the next few days, he would not _____.

12. The inventor has come up with many spectacular ideas before, but we are still awaiting his _____.

13. The _____ committed by government officials will have negative consequences for the future.

14. Captain Porter's _____ sailboat was decorated in gold and pearls.

Exercise III. Choose the set of words that best completes the sentence.

1. While crossing the river may be _____, it will require so much _____ preparation that it may hardly be worth it.
   A. feasible; laborious
   B. opulent; feasible
   C. laborious; opulent
   D. laborious; feasible

2.   Because the comedian was _____ by her audience's silence, her mind froze, and she _____ one joke for more than five minutes.
     A. opulent; elaborated
     B. belabored; discomfited
     C. discomfited; belabored
     D. laborious; elaborated

3.   Seeing the man's _____ gardens, fleet of pricey yachts, and multi-million dollar car collection, the inspector immediately suspected him of some kind of _____.
     A. laborious; magnum opus
     B. laborious; edification
     C. opulent; malfeasance
     D. feasible; lethargy

4.   The composer's _____ was a composition originally intended to provide musical accompaniment to the prayers beginning the _____.
     A. liturgy; magnum opus
     B. lethargy; edification
     C. modus operandi; liturgy
     D. magnum opus; liturgy

5.   Mother would rarely _____ on the brief statements she made regarding our clothing and choice of friends, even though she said such things for our own _____.
     A. elaborate; edification
     B. discomfit; lethargy
     C. belabor; liturgy
     D. elaborate; modus operandi

Exercise IV. Complete the sentence by inferring information about the italicized word from its context.

1.   If Rob tells the doctor that he has been feeling some *lethargy* lately, the doctor may ask if…

2.   When the restaurant critic writes admiringly about the *opulent* spread at the restaurant, he would probably note details like…

3.   Because Jen is *discomfited* by the silence in the room, she may try to…

Exercise V. Fill in each blank with the word from the Unit that best completes the sentence, using the root we supply as a clue. Then, answer the questions that follow the paragraphs.

"There is no theory. You only have to listen. Pleasure is the law." These are the words of Claude Debussy (1862-1918), French composer and founder of the Impressionist movement in music. What Debussy took pleasure in was the supreme and moving beauty of nature reflected in music. When he composed, he disregarded the harmonic style and _____ (LABOR) forms of his predecessors, the post-Wagnerians, such as Gustav Mahler and Richard Strauss. He attempted instead a kind of _____ (ERG) of music, mind, and nature that had not been heard before.

Debussy began studying piano at the age of nine, and only two years later he entered the Paris Conservatory, where he began studying composition, as well as piano. As a young adult, however, he avoided the company of musicians in favor of the leading Impressionist poets and painters, who focused on celebrating the beauty of nature in their works. "Music," Debussy wrote, "is the expression of the movement of the waters, the play of curves described by changing breezes."

In many Impressionist paintings, the colors are soft and blended, the shapes barely discernible. In fact, up close, such a painting may seem to be no more than a formless palette of colored dots. Standing back, however, one can see a pleasing image, perhaps of a river or garden. Debussy, like the painters of these works, wished to capture the subtleties of nature. He did not want his work to announce itself as a well-shaped musical composition. Instead, he wanted it to sound like an improvisation that had not been written down at all.

All of this anti-effort resulted in compositions with titles like "What the West Wind Saw," "Dead Leaves," "Sounds and Scents Revolve in the Evening Air," and a _____ (OPUS) called "La Mer" (The Sea). The last has a mysterious, dreamlike quality—some have said as puzzling and changeable as the sea itself. One can imagine Debussy descending into a reverie to write it, mimicking the spontaneous, fleeting qualities of nature, as he searched for musical notes and rhythms.

He also enjoyed composing works based on the poems of his friends. His first important orchestral work, "Prelude to the Afternoon of a Faun," was inspired by Stéphane Mallarmé's poem "L' Après-midi d'un faune."

Debussy wrote, "Beauty must appeal to the sense, must provide us with immediate enjoyment, must impress or insinuate itself into us without any effort on our part." Seemingly effortless musical beauty is Debussy's legacy. One only need hear "Clair de Lune"—a beautiful and understated piano piece—once to be convinced of that and to be grateful that Debussy dedicated his life to translating visual beauty into musical compositions.

1. The main point of this passage is that
    A. Debussy was an innovator.
    B. Debussy rejected the musical traditions of his forebears.
    C. Debussy's musical style was inspired by his love of nature.
    D. beauty must appeal to the senses.

2. Debussy was most positively influenced by
    A. his teachers at the Paris Conservatory.
    B. the Impressionist poets and painters.
    C. the post-Wagnerians Gustav Mahler and Richard Strauss.
    D. "What the West Wind Saw."

3. Based on this essay, one might conclude that Debussy believed that
    A. he would be an important influence on twentieth-century music.
    B. his teachers at the Paris Conservatory disliked his style of music.
    C. to feel the supreme and moving beauty of nature is almost like prayer.
    D. to be a great musician, he would have to be different from others.

4. The best title for this essay would be
    A. Why Debussy Rejected His Musical Past.
    B. Debussy's Influence on the Twentieth Century.
    C. Debussy: Translating Feeling into Sound.
    D. What Debussy Discovered.

Exercise VI. Drawing on your knowledge of roots and words in context, read the following selection and define the italicized words. If you cannot figure out the meaning of the words on your own, look them up in a dictionary. Note that in this case, *ef*, from *ex*, means "out from."

Greeling Helicopter Manufacturing is currently in the final stages of testing the new TG-45 helicopter. The designers promise a much more *ergonomic* seat and dashboard arrangement, which will allow the pilot to maximize attention to in-flight controls. The motor-uptake system in the TG-45 is said to be far more *efficacious* for short-range flights, delivering reliable bursts of power while minimizing energy use.

UNIT TWO

STA, STI
Latin STARE, STANTUM, "to stand; to stay"

STANCH (stânch) *v.* to stop the flow of
Desperate to *stanch* the blood seeping from the wound, the doctor decided to put a tourniquet on the patient's arm above the elbow.
syn: cease

STAUNCH (stônch) *adj.* firm and steadfast
Though Reverend Lockwood was a *staunch* believer in the goodness of humanity, he found his faith tested by the horrible events of that week.
syn: strong   *ant: fickle, wavering*

EXTANT (əks tânt´) *adj.* still in existence; not destroyed
L. *ex*, "from" + *stantum = staying from*
Scientists continue to search through the remains of the museum in the hopes that they will discover some *extant* works of art.
syn: existing   *ant: extinct*

RESTIVE (res´ tiv) *adj.*   1. resisting authority; difficult to control
                                 2. restless; fidgety
L. *re*, "back" + *stare = to stand back*
1. Police feared the townspeople would grow *restive* under the strict curfew and begin to engage in acts of civil disorder.
2. The elderly man expected the children to become *restive* during his long speech, but they listened attentively instead.

POS
Latin PONERE, POSITUM, "to put, to place"

APROPOS (a prə´ pō) *prep.* with regard to
L. *a*, "to, toward" + *pro*, "forth" + *positum = toward what has been put forth*
Apropos of Jim's speech on nuclear energy, Dawn mentioned that a new power plant would be built in the neighboring town.
syn: concerning   *ant: irrelevant*

DEPOSE (dē pōz´) *v.* to remove from office or power
L. *de*, "down" + *positum = to put down*
The rule of Czar Nicholas came to an end when he and other members of the royal family were *deposed* and murdered by rebel forces.
                    ant: elect

▥ *It's odd that the staunchest defenders of freedom still approve of the government's right to pick and choose where a citizen may travel.*
—Anonymous

▥ *Despite its appearance, the word* restive *has nothing to do with rest. It originally described an animal such as a horse or cow that stood back and refused to move. It now also applies to a person or group of people who are difficult to control.*

STAS, STAT
Greek STATOS, "standing"

STATIC   (staʹ tək)   *adj.*   having no motion or change
Critics found the composer's latest work *static*, boring, and lacking in emotional development.
syn: still   *ant: dynamic*

ECSTASY   (ekʹ stə sē)   *n.*   an intense joy or delight
G. *ec*, "out of" + *stasis* = *standing outside (one's body)*
The *ecstasy* Bob felt after watching the Yankees win the World Series was matched only by his joy at the birth of his daughter.
syn: elation   *ant: misery*

STASIS   (stāʹ sis)   *n.*   a condition in which there is no change
Scientists find it difficult to accurately predict climate patterns because the environment is not in *stasis*, but constantly changing.
syn: equilibrium, balance

ENT, ESS
Latin ESSE, "to be"

ENTITY   (enʹ ti tē)   *n.*   a being
For tax purposes, a married couple may be considered either two people or a single *entity*.

ESSENCE   (éʹ səns)   *n.*   the most important ingredient; the crucial element
After months of preparation, the lawyers finally began to discuss the *essence* of the case.
syn: crux

QUINTESSENTIAL   (kwin tə sənʹ shəl)   *adj.*   the most typical, ideal, or important
L. *quintus*, "fifth" + *esse* = *the fifth state of being; the fifth essence*
The goalie declared that the Rangers' victory in the last second of the final game was his *quintessential* sports triumph.
syn: ultimate

We watched the QUEEN'S ASCENT up Everest, the QUINTESSENTIAL mountain.

III *Everyone has heard of static* electricity, *but what do you think it means, based on its definition of "having no motion"?*

III *In ancient and medieval philosophy, quintessence was the fifth and highest essence, after the four elements of earth, air, fire, and water. It was thought to be the substance of the heavenly bodies and present in all things. The word now describes the purest form or instance of something.*

EXERCISES - UNIT TWO

Exercise I. Complete the sentence in a way that shows you understand the meaning of the italicized vocabulary word.

1. A group of local citizens has drafted a petition to *depose* the governor on the grounds that...

2. Peter was such a *staunch* supporter of his local youth orchestra that he often...

3. Because the manuscripts are the only *extant* writings from the time of the town's founding, we can assume...

4. Nate began to grow *restive* when his parents...

5. The rainforest finally achieved some *stasis* when...

6. Trying to *stanch* the influx of invasive species into the country, the government...

7. The fresh roses seemed the *quintessential* expression of love because...

8. The *ecstasy* that the spelling-bee contestant felt was the result of...

9. Julie's comments about the class were completely *apropos* because she...

10. The business group was not a legal *entity* because...

11. The *essence* of the manufacturer's speech against taxes on trade was that...

12. Feeling that his existence had become rather *static*, Jay decided to...

Exercise II. Fill in the blank with the best word from the choices below. One word will not be used.

       quintessential   extant   apropos   static   entity

1. Though technology has brought great change to other towns, Avondale has remained
_____.

2. During his quest to find the _____ elements of wisdom, Robert gradually learned that no human being has the answers.

3. Of the thousands of works that the composer wrote, only six are still _____.

4. _____ of what we were discussing, have you had a ride on the new carousel?

Fill in the blank with the best word from the choices below. One word will not be used.

staunch   restive   ecstasy   stanch   depose

5.   The puppy, growing _____ in his snug harness, began to squirm and bark.

6.   Fearing that her subjects might _____ her, the queen began repealing some of her stricter laws.

7.   Once a roomful of infants has started crying, no one can _____ the flood of tears.

8.   As they realized their team was about to win the championship, the fans leaped to their feet in _____.

Fill in the blank with the best word from the choices below. One word will not be used.

staunch   stasis   essence   entity   stanch

9.   What appeared to be a period of _____ for the musician was actually a time of great internal change.

10. The Martians' leader seemed to be a(n) _____ of great power and knowledge.

11. The true _____ of the opera's magnificence is captured for the first time on this recording.

12. Although I considered myself a(n) _____ defender of my religion, I knew that others were far more devoted.

Exercise III. Choose the set of words that best completes the sentence.

1.   The subjects of the king grew _____ under his strict control and threatened to rise up and _____ him.
     A. static; staunch
     B. restive; depose
     C. apropos; stanch
     D. extant; depose

2.   Certain religions teach that, while the world gives the appearance of movement and change, the _____ of existence is actually _____ and permanent.
     A. entity; staunch
     B. quintessence; apropos
     C. ecstasy; extant
     D. essence; static

3.   _____ of the question about political parties, Marty reminded everyone that he was a(n) _____ supporter
        of candidate Reynolds.
        A. Staunch; extant
        B. Apropos; staunch
        C. Extant; restive
        D. Quintessential; stanch

4.   "Surely," said Sean in total _____, "this is the _____ of a perfect meal."
        A. entity; essence
        B. essence; stasis
        C. ecstasy; stasis
        D. ecstasy; quintessence

5.   The _____ literature about the long-dead civilization's government seems to describe the court as a(n)
        _____ separate from the king's cabinet.
        A. static; essence
        B. extant; entity
        C. apropos; quintessence
        D. staunch; entity

Exercise IV. Complete the sentence by inferring information about the italicized word from its context.

1.   Tim was in *ecstasy* after the chemistry exam, so we can guess that he…

2.   If Trina says that only five of the ancient art works are *extant*, we can infer that the rest…

3.   If the members of the swim team vote to *depose* their squad leader, it may be because…

**Exercise V. Fill in each blank with the word from the Unit that best completes the sentence, using the root
we supply as a clue. Then, answer the questions that follow the paragraphs.**

Water is not only the _____ (ESS) of life, but also one of the greatest forces of nature. It covers most of the earth's surface (approximately 67%), and its constant movement, through a process called *erosion*, shapes continents and carves out rivers and lakes. Nowhere is the force of this process more evident than in the Grand Canyon.

Called one of the Seven Wonders of the Natural World, the Grand Canyon, in northern Arizona, is a 277-mile-long gorge created by millennia of erosion from the Colorado River. Because of the desert climate, the soil in the canyon is hard; it doesn't absorb liquids. When it rains in the Southwest, it often does so in torrents, sparking flash floods, which force water over the desert surface quickly, removing soil. With no deep-rooted plants to keep the soil in place, a higher volume of dirt and debris washes away, trimming another layer from the canyon.

In the spring, the Colorado River also carries snowmelt from the Rocky Mountains; these annual floods wash particles of stone and dirt from the highest peaks to the Pacific Ocean. The river also brings an annual influx of thrill-seekers, people riding the rapids in inflatable rafts, enjoying nature's own roller coaster.

However, a series of dams interposed at various points on the river have disrupted its once-mighty flow. In a dammed river, erosion still occurs, but at a slower pace. A reduced current has made it difficult for the river to move larger rocks and sediment; debris that would have been washed away now remains. The riverbed is becoming congested.

Water, however, will find its way around any obstacle. The Colorado River has widened, reducing its banks and cutting into the canyon walls. Slower-moving water has also allowed some _____ (STAT) ponds to develop.

This water seeps beneath the canyon floor, penetrating layers of rock it hadn't touched before. The consequences of this process are not yet fully understood.

Ice also affects the canyon. Because of the Grand Canyon's elevation, winter weather conditions are in effect despite the desert setting. Snow and ice are common. When water freezes in cracks and crevices along the canyon walls, it expands the rock, splitting off pieces that fall to the canyon floor, washing away or creating more obstacles.

The Grand Canyon took centuries to mold, and it continues to change, yet this progression is barely noticeable during the average person's lifespan. The alteration takes place one speck of dirt at a time. Human intervention, however, takes only moments to alter the mighty canyon.

1.   What made the Grand Canyon?
     A.   rocks and dirt
     B.   people and machines
     C.   earthquakes
     D.   water and erosion

2.   What is the primary reason erosion has been slowed in the canyon?
     A.   less rain
     B.   dams on the river
     C.   construction of breakers and walls
     D.   snow melt

3.   What causes standing pools in the river?
     A.   water seeping under the canyon floor
     B.   gravity
     C.   an influx of thrill-seekers
     D.   the slowing of water by the dams

4.   Which of the following is a characteristic of erosion?
     A.   stagnant ponds
     B.   a bend in the river
     C.   flash flooding
     D.   removal of dirt and debris

Exercise VI. Drawing on your knowledge of roots and words in context, read the following selection and define the italicized words. If you cannot figure out the meaning of the words on your own, look them up in a dictionary. Note that *de* means "down" and *apo* means "away from."

The priest was called upon to give a *deposition* in a civil trial. Because his testimony helped put a frequent lawbreaker behind bars, the priest was commended by the district attorney. However, in speaking to the court, the priest revealed beliefs that were in opposition to those of his supervisors. He was subsequently accused of *apostasy* in a separate Church hearing.

UNIT THREE

VERD, VIRID
Latin VIRIDUS, "green"

VERDURE (ver´ dyər) *n.* greenery; fresh and ripe vegetation
For decades, tourists have visited the botanical garden to marvel at its astonishing *verdure*.
syn: foliage

VERDANT (ver´ dənt) *adj.* green; lush with vegetation
Because of the sunny days, the land was *verdant*, and the harvest was full.
ant: barren

VIRIDITY (və rid´ ə tē) *n.* a lack of experience; an innocence
Quentin's *viridity* was a sure sign that he had led a very sheltered life.

CAND
Latin CANDIDUS, "white; pure"
Latin CANDERE, CANDITUM, "to glow; to burn"

CANDID (kân´ did) *adj.* open and sincere
In my home, I gave the film crew my *candid* opinion about the matter.
syn: frank   *ant: duplicitous*

CANDOR (kân´ dər) *n.* a frankness or sincerity of expression; an openness
Donald showed a *candor* that was unique among the politicians in the race.
syn: truth   *ant: falseness*

INCANDESCENT (in kən de´ sənt) *adj.* shining brilliantly
L. *in*, "very" + *candere = glowing intensely*
The actress's *incandescent* gold gown was the talk of all the celebrities at the awards ceremony last night.

In Latin, as in English, the color green was associated with youth and inexperience.

In ancient Rome, a man running for office was distinguished by his white (candidus) toga, a symbol of purity and honesty. He was known as a candidatus. Our modern-day candidates are no longer required to wear white, but they strive in the same way to convey an image of sincerity.

PALL
Latin PALLERE, "to be pale"

PALLOR (pa´lər) *n.* an extreme or unnatural paleness
The guilty man's face took on a distinct *pallor*, and his hands began to tremble.
ant: flushed

PALLID (pa´ləd) *adj.* lacking color; dull
Patrick knew that Juliette was sick when he saw the young girl's *pallid* face.
syn: wan

APPALL (ə pawl´) *v.* to fill with horror or disapproval
L. *ad*, "toward" + *pallere* = *toward paleness*
Karl was *appalled* to learn that the beautiful old museum was going to be replaced by a shopping mall.
syn: horrify

When the corpse sat up, the PALLBEARERS were APPALLED.

LIVID
Latin LIVIDUS, "bluish-black"

LIVID (li´vid) *adj.* enraged; furious
When the salesperson demanded that I return what I had "stolen," I became *livid* and threatened to sue.

NIGR
Latin NIGER, "black"

DENIGRATE (de´ni grāt) *v.* to attack the character of; to mock
L. *de*, "very" + *niger* = *to intensely blacken (the reputation of)*
The notoriously harsh theatre critic rarely hesitated to *denigrate* even the most famous and respected actors.
syn: belittle   *ant: praise*

▥ Palladium, *a silvery-gray metal that has similar chemical properties to platinum, is named after the Roman goddess* Pallas (Athena).

▥ *Though* lavender *may not be seen as an especially angry color, it has a connection to* livid. *Both words come from the Latin term for a purplish color that is between blue and black.*

EXERCISES - UNIT THREE

Exercise I. Complete the sentence in a way that shows you understand the meaning of the italicized vocabulary word.

1. Philip was so *appalled* by the hospital's condition that he...

2. Though the garden had once been strikingly *verdant*, it was now...

3. Paulina's natural tendency to be very *candid* sometimes makes other people...

4. The *pallor* of John's complexion finally went away when...

5. Andre's habit of *denigrating* his coworkers earned him a reputation as...

6. The retreating soldiers' faces were *pallid* because...

7. When the weary, thirsty travelers saw the *verdure* of the land they were approaching, they...

8. Rather than explaining with *candor* why he was firing Lucy, Mike...

9. Dirk was so *livid* about the loss of his favorite painting that he seemed ready to...

10. The *incandescent* city skyline stood in sharp contrast to...

11. When the anthropologist stumbled on a never-before-seen tribe in the middle of Brazil's jungle, he expected to find simple *viridity* among the people, but instead...

Exercise II. Fill in the blank with the best word from the choices below. One word will not be used.

pallor	candor	livid	verdant

1. Though we don't know if Trina really did see a ghost, the _____ of her face tells us that something scared her.

2. Was the golf course a _____ oasis in the middle of a busy city, or just an overly landscaped playground for the wealthy?

3. The state trooper had seen many people involved in minor accidents get angry, but none had become as _____ as the woman whose car was barely scratched.

Fill in the blank with the best word from the choices below. One word will not be used.

candid   viridity   appall   candor   pallid

4. Even Governor Ling, known as a man of great _____, did not give a straightforward answer about the controversial issue.

5. The chief of police said that she was _____ by citizens' lack of respect for even the most basic laws.

6. When bringing up the problems you have with your roommate, it is best to be _____ and sincere, but not insulting or aggressive.

7. Malcolm's short story has a modern plot: a strong, fearless, and intelligent woman defeats the villain, who had thought her facade of _____ and naïveté were real.

Fill in the blank with the best word from the choices below. One word will not be used.

verdure   livid   denigrate   incandescent   pallid

8. Corinne's red hair, catching the afternoon sunlight, seemed almost _____.

9. Though he admitted that the _____ of the meadows was pleasing to the eye, Anthony missed his home in the Painted Desert.

10. Some of the children in the ward regained mobility and their former youthful glow, while others remained _____ and almost lifeless.

11. Even when people _____ her skills, Ashley enjoys playing volleyball.

Exercise III. Choose the set of words that best completes the sentence.

1. We were _____ by the transformation of the forest's untouched _____ into polluted streets and overcrowded shopping centers.
    A. denigrated; candor
    B. appalled; verdure
    C. livid; pallor
    D. denigrated; verdure

2. The island's _____ palm trees were framed by the _____ orange of the setting sun.
    A. candid; verdant
    B. livid; pallid
    C. verdant; incandescent
    D. incandescent; livid

3. Tracy wished she could speak with _____ to her coworker without having him turn _____ and storm out of the office.
    A. viridity; pallid
    B. candor; livid
    C. pallor; incandescent
    D. verdure; livid

4. When the doctor saw the sickly _____ of the patient's face, he made the _____ pronouncement that death was surely not long off.
    A. viridity; livid
    B. verdure; candid
    C. pallor; incandescent
    D. pallor; candid

5. Anne's super-athletic brother _____ her by saying she had "no muscles, a(n) _____ complexion, and a complete lack of knowledge of sports."
    A. appalled; pallid
    B. denigrated; pallid
    C. appalled; incandescent
    D. denigrated; verdant

Exercise IV. Complete the sentence by inferring information about the italicized word from its context.

1. If Haley *denigrates* her younger siblings on a regular basis, they may feel…

2. If Corinne wants to transform the vacant lot into a *verdant* space, she should probably start by…

3. Sari may infer that her brother is *livid* when he does things like…

Exercise V. Fill in each blank with the word from the Unit that best completes the sentence, using the root we supply as a clue. Then, answer the questions that follow the paragraphs.

Industrialized society's continued expansion has triggered both positive and negative effects on the surrounding environment. Some feel that the lumber industry, in particular, has repeatedly devastated and reconstructed ecosystems simply in order to satisfy humanity's wants and needs. This is fallacious reasoning, however; the lumber industry does not proceed with reckless abandon. Logging merely serves to satisfy consumer demands. To be _____ (CAND), this business rarely receives the recognition it deserves for its tremendous contributions to reforestation.

One location perfectly demonstrating this trend is the Pacific Northwest. High in the Cascades, millions of acres of lush forest have been razed to supply the timber demand throughout the world. Once covered with thick, dense _____ (VERD), the mountains now exhibit large bare patches—dismal symbols, seemingly, of human disregard for nature. Upon closer inspection, though, one will find energetic young forests sprouting from seedlings planted by the logging businesses themselves. These businesses admit with _____ (CAND) that past practices have harmed the environment, but they now feel that the only responsible act would be to restore what they removed, especially when numerous studies have delineated the role that trees play in reducing pollution.

Through photosynthesis, trees and other types of vegetation serve as filters, removing carbon dioxides from the air and offering a protective umbrella to the life below. When a portion of a forest is removed, the undergrowth perishes, and the animals supported by that habitat must leave. Lacking the necessary protection, an entire ecosystem succumbs to humanity's needs. In spite of this bleak consequence, the lumber industry does not abandon the lingering destruction;

instead, it undertakes the massive task of rebuilding what nature created.

What should be strikingly _____ (PALL) in this situation is the fact that the majority of the blame falls upon the lumber industry; consequently, the primary reforestation effort is designated as the industry's obligation. Granted, these businesses bear direct responsibility for leveling forests, but they commit this act for consumers, who need the wood to build homes, offices, furniture, playground equipment, and many more commodities that enhance everyday life. Perhaps the growing social conscience in today's world should acknowledge that, since many consume what the planet supplies, many shoulder the duty of replenishing the environment. Society needs to assume a greater role in restoring the balance between nature and industry. Blame accomplishes nothing, but shared responsibility and effort make a tremendous difference.

1. The author's tone toward industry could best be described as
   A. supportive.
   B. disgusted.
   C. aggressive.
   D. dismayed.

2. Which sentence best states the main idea of this passage?
   A. The Industrial Revolution has slowly destroyed the environment.
   B. The lumber industry is responsible for the damage it has caused; therefore, it should assume the task of reforestation.
   C. The lumber industry has received too much blame for deforestation and not enough credit for restoration.
   D. Trees are a necessary part of most ecosystems, and the lumber industry has effectively destroyed irreplaceable habitats.

3. The author claims that the lumber industry has failed to receive recognition for
   A. meeting increased demand.
   B. providing alternatives to wood building supplies.
   C. following strict guidelines.
   D. attempting to restore habitats.

4. According to the passage, restoring forests is important because
   A. animals require specific habitats, and deforestation leads to extinction.
   B. the forest supports many lives by protecting undergrowth and reducing pollution.
   C. logging businesses are attempting to avoid negative publicity resulting from their impact on nature.
   D. such a great demand exists for wood products that economic disaster would occur if forests were not restored.

Exercise VI. Drawing on your knowledge of roots and words in context, read the following selection and define the italicized words. If you cannot figure out the meaning of the words on your own, look them up in a dictionary.

The center of the blossom is *viridescent* in early spring, but by the middle of May, most of the green has darkened to purplish-blue. The flowers have an industrial, as well as decorative use because they become *candent* at an unusually low temperature. Their capacity to burn may lead to more efficient lighting systems as researchers better understand the properties of the plant.

UNIT FOUR

PECC

Latin PECCARE, PECCATUM, "to sin; to be flawed"

PECCADILLO   (pə kə di´ lō)   *n.*   a small sin or fault
Leonard grew so irritated by his roommate's *peccadilloes* that he threatened to move out.

IMPECCABLE   (im pek´ ə bəl)   *adj.*   having no flaws
L. *in*, "not" + *peccare* = *not sinning*
Oliver's *impeccable* comic timing made him the center of every party.
syn: perfect   *ant: flawed*

PECCANT   (pe´ kənt)   *adj.*   violating a moral law; sinful
The seamstress was exiled from the colony for her supposedly *peccant* activity.

PEJ, PAIR

Latin PEJOR, "worse"

PEJORATIVE   (pe jôr´ ə tiv)   *adj.*   negative and critical; insulting
Mosheh was clearly disturbed by the *pejorative* comments used in the review of his latest album.
syn: belittling, derogatory   *ant: praising*

IMPAIR   (im pâr´)   *v.*   to cause to diminish in strength, value, or quality
L. *in*, "in" + *pejor* = *(to cause to be) in worse condition*
A new report claims that many prescription drugs will severely *impair* one's ability to operate a vehicle.
syn: harm   *ant: fix*

III Peccadillo *entered English from Spanish. The -illo suffix means "little, small."*

III Impair *is another word that came to English through French. One syllable dropped out of the original* pejor *root, but the meaning of the word is still closely related to its etymological ancestor.*

MAL
Latin MALUS, "bad"

MALIGN   (mə līn´)   *v.*   to speak of maliciously; to insult
L. *malus + gignus,* "nature" = *bad-natured; to act bad-naturedly*
The pamphlet tried to help the incumbent win the re-election race for city council by *maligning* the two opposing candidates.
syn: deprecate   *ant: praise*

MALINGER   (mə lin´ gər)   *v.*   to pretend to be sick in order to avoid something
Shannon *malingered* all day Friday because she hadn't studied for her math test.
syn: shirk

MALAISE   (mə lāz´)   *n.*   a sense of unease; depression
One year after the crash of the stock market, the economy remains stuck in a deep *malaise.*
syn: melancholy

Boring PLAYS = Audience MALAISE

NEG
Latin NEGARE, NEGATUM, "to deny"
Latin NEGLEGERE, "to neglect"

NEGLIGENT   (ne´ glə jənt)   *adj.*   not properly attentive
Because the captain had been *negligent* in his maintenance of the ship, the hull developed a leak.
syn: careless   *ant: careful, attentive*

NEGLIGIBLE   (ne´ gli ji bəl)   *adj.*   unimportant; insignificant
L. *neglegere + ible,* "able" = *able to be neglected*
Although the automobile accident was terrifying, actual damage to the car was *negligible.*
syn: minor, trivial   *ant: worthwhile*

NEGATE   (nə gāt´)   *v.*   to cancel the effect of; to nullify
Donna feared that her years of gymnastics training would be *negated* by an accident during the competition.
syn: deny, contradict   *ant: affirm*

▥ *Nothing cures the day-to-day* malaise *better than falling head-over-heels in love with the right person.*
—Anonymous

▥ *A renegade was originally someone who denied the principles of the Catholic Church.*

EXERCISES - UNIT FOUR

Exercise I. Complete the sentence in a way that shows you understand the meaning of the italicized vocabulary word.

1.   The general *malaise* of workers who flipped burgers all day was probably caused by…

2.   People who saw it used *pejorative* language when describing the film because…

3.   Patty hoped that the good work she did at the soup kitchen would not be *negated* by…

4.   Omar's *impeccable* manners make anyone who dines with him feel…

5.   Daniel's ability to take the test was *impaired* by…

6.   In an attempt to *malign* Sally, the attorney who was questioning her said…

7.   Because the chief of the construction crew was *negligent* when it came to safety standards…

8.   Charlene feels that her lying is a *peccadillo* rather than…

9.   When Jackie saw that the damage to her house from the storm was *negligible*, she…

10.   My mother accused my brother and me of *malingering* when we…

11.   The priest urged any *peccant* churchgoers to…

Exercise II. Fill in the blank with the best word from the choices below. One word will not be used.

peccadillo   negligible   impeccable   malaise

1.   In order to get along in the cramped cabin, we had to ignore one another's _____.

2.   After the series of economic and natural disasters, many citizens of Squalley's Gulch fell into a deep
      _____.

3.   The effect of Chemical X on the human brain was once thought disastrous, but it is now considered
      _____.

Fill in the blank with the best word from the choices below. One word will not be used.

malign	negligent	pejorative	malinger	impeccable

4.   Leigh explained that her remark was not meant to be _____, regardless of how offensive it had sounded.

5.   Andy's _____ study skills ensured that he never missed a day's homework.

6.   Although other writers _____ Craig for his strange style, he continues to write in an experimental fashion.

7.   Stu's habitual _____ exasperated his boss and cost Stu his job.

Fill in the blank with the best word from the choices below. One word will not be used.

negligible	impair	negligent	peccant	negate

8.   Studies have found that missing breakfast in the morning may _____ a child's ability to pay attention in class.

9.   A(n) _____ camper had left a pit fire burning, and the flames soon spread to the nearby forest.

10.   The nun scolded her group of children, warning them to mend their _____ ways.

11.   Molly's mother advised her that all the regret in the world could not _____ a hurtful word or deed.

Exercise III. Choose the set of words that best completes the sentence.

1.   The counselor says that minor flaws and _____ may be considered _____, but they can lead to greater problems in a marriage.
     A.   malaise; negligent
     B.   peccadilloes; negligible
     C.   pejoratives; impeccable
     D.   malaise; pejorative

2.   Charlie was shocked to find his _____ academic record _____ by a hostile professor.
     A.   negligent; negated
     B.   peccant; malingered
     C.   impeccable; maligned
     D.   negligible; impaired

3.   The _____ that Ivan had been suffering for weeks made it difficult for him to pay attention; as a result,
      he was _____ in several areas of his job.
      A. peccadillo; negligible
      B. peccant; pejorative
      C. malaise; impeccable
      D. malaise; negligent

4.   Was Steve's ability to walk really _____, or was he simply _____ to get out of any heavy lifting?
      A. negated; maligning
      B. peccant; impairing
      C. negligent; malingering
      D. impaired; malingering

5.   No amount of flattery can _____ the hurtful and _____ term you used to describe me.
      A. negate; pejorative
      B. impair; peccant
      C. malinger; negligent
      D. malign; negligible

Exercise IV. Complete the sentence by inferring information about the italicized word from its context.

1.   When Iggy begins listing some of Meredith's *peccadilloes*, Meredith will probably feel…

2.   If Horatio is *negligent* in his gardening duties, the flowers may…

3.   If Tamara wants to get out from under her *malaise*, she should try to…

**Exercise V. Fill in each blank with the word from the Unit that best completes the sentence, using the root
      we supply as a clue. Then, answer the questions that follow the paragraphs.**

As spring approaches each year, millions of avid backyard gardeners stream into local hardware stores and nurseries, while others pore over catalogues and scour the Internet in a relentless quest to create a(n) _____ (PECC) garden. These people take time from their busy schedules to share in a primal, soothing activity: creating beauty and sustenance by joining forces with nature.

Establishing a worthy garden is not a simple task; it requires dedicated planning and constant attention. Choosing the appropriate seeds and plants demands knowledge of climate, soil, sunlight, and drainage conditions. Sometimes, gardeners must also devise blueprints detailing specific positioning of plants in the garden, as certain plants need or deplete certain minerals. Gardeners must also turn the soil, mixing it with a nutrient-rich growing medium to replenish necessary resources. Once physically structured, the garden is ready for planting.

Many gardeners pay careful attention to the preparation of their seeds. They begin the growing period indoors, usually six to eight weeks before spring. This produces sturdy plants ready for transplanting outdoors; however, transferring the seedlings is a delicate process. Relocating plants too hastily may _____ (PAIR) their ability to grow and thrive in a new environment. To avoid this dilemma, many gardeners place seedlings outside in the daylight and shelter them overnight for one to two weeks prior to transplanting. Seeds planted directly in the garden require slightly less care because this process does not entail an adjustment period. Whether the garden consists of plants grown inside or outside, it still needs daily attention once established.

A _____ (NEG) gardener, who fails to water or weed the garden, will find the plants wilting and starving for nutrients. Most garden plants do not tolerate drought conditions, but weeds can thrive in such situations, stealing whatever nourishment they require from the other vegetation. Devoted gardeners would never cause such harm to their masterpieces. They diligently clear weeds, provide fertilizer, and deliver moisture as their precious plants command; as a result, they produce lush, healthy, fruitful gardens.

Gardening is a time-consuming and demanding, yet rewarding diversion. Producing sturdy, flourishing, and productive plants provides immense satisfaction and a grand sense of accomplishment. Few other activities in today's busy world share such rewards.

1.   According to the passage, a successful gardener is
      A. persistent and stubborn.
      B. dedicated and knowledgeable.
      C. patient and nimble.
      D. meticulous and diplomatic.

2.   Why must a gardener clear weeds from the garden, according to the article?
      A. The weeds block sunlight from the seedlings.
      B. The weeds tangle around the garden plants and stunt their growth.
      C. The weeds deplete the soil of important nutrients.
      D. The weeds infect the garden plants with mold.

3.   According to the author, plants that use up minerals
      A. specifically position the soil in the garden.
      B. must have a particular location in the garden.
      C. must be mixed with a richer soil.
      D. require constant attention.

Exercise VI. Drawing on your knowledge of roots and words in context, read the following selection and define the italicized words. If you cannot figure out the meaning of the words on your own, look them up in a dictionary. Note that *fac* means "make" and *ab* means "from."

Although some have seen Prince Mikhail as the greatest *malefactor* in the tiny country's troubled history, recent scholarship has shown that some of his deeds were not so terrible for the well-being of his subjects as previously thought. Then, too, when he decided he was unfit to rule, he immediately *abnegated* control. Surely, the sacrifice of power for the nation's greater good redeems him, despite his mistakes.

UNIT FIVE

JOC
Latin JOCUS, "joke"

JOCOSE (jə kōs´) *adj.* cheerful; merry
The *jocose* language of the play is a reflection of the playwright's youthful optimism.
syn: happy, mirthful   *ant: morose*

JOCULAR (jo´ kū lər) *adj.* characterized by joking
When the normally serious brothers got together, their language became *jocular* and playful.
syn: jovial

The JOCULAR JOCK gave his coach bunny ears in the team photo.

> III *Note that the word* jocose *does not need to be connected to joking; it can refer to something that is enjoyable or happy, like an evening or a mood.*

FEST, FET
Latin FESTUS, "festive"

FESTOON (fəs tōōn´) *v.* to drape or adorn festively
During the holidays, the rafters of the old house were *festooned* with flowers and ribbons.

FETE (fāt) *v.* to honor with a banquet or feast
For her 80th birthday, Mrs. Okapi was *feted* by her many friends and admirers.
syn: celebrate

BACCH
From the name of the Roman god of wine and celebration, BACCHUS

BACCHIC (bäk´ ək) *adj.* of or related to a wild celebration
The policeman reported that he had stumbled upon a *bacchic* gathering in the woods near the high school.

BACCHANAL (bäk´ ə näl) *n.* a drunken party or celebration
Greg's graduation party turned into a wild *bacchanal* when his rowdy friend Mike showed up.

> III *Bacchus was associated not only with celebration and festivity, but also with loss of emotional control due to heightened intensity of experience. So, if you hear something described as "Bacchic," think of a party raging wildly out of control.*

PLAINT
Latin PLANGERE, PLANCTUS, "to lament"

PLAINTIVE (plān´ təv) *adj.*   sorrowful; expressing or evoking mourning
or sadness
The *plaintive* notes of the trumpet playing "Taps" floated over the funeral
procession.
ant: joyful

PLAINT (plānt) *n.*   a lament or complaint
Despite the *plaint* of the opera's heroine, the soldier she loves returns to battle.

ELEG
Greek ELEGOS, "song of lament"

ELEGY (el´ ə jē) *n.*   a song or poem memorializing something or someone
Louis and Debbie had never been very close, so everyone was surprised when he
wrote a lovely *elegy* for her after her untimely death.

ELEGIAC (el ə jē´ ək) *adj.*   mourning that which is lost or past; sorrowful
Dave's stories about his childhood took on a distinctly *elegiac* tone whenever they
involved the loss of his two dogs in a car accident.
syn: mournful

III *The plaintiff in a legal case is someone who has a grievance or complaint; the defendant must answer the plaintiff's charges.*

III *Both elegiac and elegy have to do with loss, with something slipping away, and with sadness. In addition, they also convey the idea of beauty.*

EXERCISES - UNIT FIVE

Exercise I. Complete the sentence in a way that shows you understand the meaning of the italicized vocabulary word.

1.   The members of the garden club were in a *jocose* mood because…

2.   The poet's *plaint* about his true love was inspired by…

3.   The employees *festooned* the office with crepe paper because…

4.   The quiet dinner gathering quickly became a *bacchanal* when…

5.   The *elegiac* tone of the speech my father gave at my wedding made it clear that he felt…

6.   Dewey often fantasized about being *feted* for his…

7.   As the participants in the *bacchic* procession moved along, they…

8.   Millie's *plaintive* song made many in the audience think of…

9.   Being of a naturally *jocular* disposition, Lloyd often…

10.   In Barbara's *elegy* for her departed teacher, she says that…

Exercise II. Fill in the blank with the best word from the choices below. One word will not be used.

      jocose   fete   elegiac   festoon

1.   The director tried desperately to get his depressed actors into the _____ mood they needed for the party scene.

2.   The film ends on a(n) _____ note: the main character, recalling all the friends he has lost, sheds a single tear.

3.   The sailboat was _____ with lights for the Bon Voyage banquet.

Fill in the blank with the best word from the choices below. One word will not be used.

      plaint   bacchanal   elegy   plaintive   fete

4.   A(n) _____ sob entered Beth's voice as she described her lost cat.

5.   As a freshman in college, Bill was always ready to party all night at one of the _____ thrown by his unruly classmates.

6.   Ignoring the _____ of the lovesick young man below her balcony, Andrea focused her telescope on a particular star.

7.   Bobo and Chuckles _____ the founder of their organization with a splendid dinner at the Clown Club.

Fill in the blank with the best word from the choices below. One word will not be used.

      elegiac   bacchic   jocular   elegy

8.   When Paris was liberated from the Nazis, crowds of people celebrated with _____ abandon.

9.   To honor the death of the soldiers, the musician recast one of his more popular tunes as a(n) _____ expressing sorrow and loss.

10.   Janice said sternly that she did not appreciate our _____ behavior during what should have been a very solemn occasion.

Exercise III. Choose the set of words that best completes the sentence.

1.   Lionel had entitled his poem "A(n) _____ Against My Cruel Girlfriend," but his _____ tone made it clear that he really felt no ill will.
    A. Fete; jocular
    B. Elegy; plaintive
    C. Plaint; jocular
    D. Bacchanal; jocose

2.   _____ partygoers, laughing and dancing, wandered here and there in the great hall, which was _____ with strings of flowers.
    A. Jocose; festooned
    B. Plaintive; feted
    C. Elegiac; plaintive
    D. Bacchic; feted

3. The beloved leader had often been _____ by adoring followers during his life; now, in death, he was memorialized in a touching _____.
   A. festooned; elegy
   B. feted; elegy
   C. plaintive; bacchanal
   D. jocose; fete

4. The author's _____ last book concludes that even the most glorious _____ of youth are brought to an end by sorrow and loss.
   A. plaintive; elegies
   B. jocose; bacchanals
   C. bacchic; fetes
   D. elegiac; bacchanals

5. In the midst of the _____ celebration in the town square, a(n) _____ and terrible cry was heard coming from the hills.
   A. bacchic; plaintive
   B. jocular; elegiac
   C. plaintive; jocose
   D. festooned; plaintive

Exercise IV. Complete the sentence by inferring information about the italicized word from its context.

1. If Roberta chooses to open her concert with a *plaintive* ballad, she may be feeling…

2. When Carl is *feted* by people who were once hostile to him, he may wonder if…

3. Because Nicolas has a naturally *jocose* personality, he often makes other people feel…

Exercise V. Fill in each blank with the word from the Unit that best completes the sentence, using the root we supply as a clue. Then, answer the questions that follow the paragraphs.

A bee gathers pollen from a flower and returns to her hive. When she meets another bee, she begins to move from side to side and walk forward and around in an odd way. As she walks, she vibrates rapidly back and forth. She repeats her strange moves several times.

A kind of kingfisher known as the Laughing Kookaburra lives in the trees of an Australian forest. The bird gets its name from the sound of its call, which resembles human laughter.

We might imagine that the bee is dancing for joy—maybe she is in the middle of some kind of _____ (BACCH) frenzy. Maybe the bird is always in a _____ (JOC) mood. But these are human emotions, and we have no way of knowing whether animals participate in the same experiences. When we assume we know how animals are "feeling," we are engaging in *anthropomorphism*.

Anthropomorphism is the tendency to see human actions and intention in the behavior of non-human organisms and objects. The word comes from two Greek roots: *anthropos*, which means "man," and *morphe*, which means "shape."

Anthropomorphism can have negative consequences for both people and animals. Animals don't have the same needs as humans; if we see them as just like us, we may do them more harm than good. For example, chimpanzees are often used in entertainment when they are young because they resemble human children. When they grow large and unmanageable, however, they must be removed from their homes and put in zoos or released back into the wild. Unskilled at living in the wild and traumatized by their separation from their human families, they are easy targets for predators or poachers.

People, on the other hand, need the "otherness" that comes from an unbiased study of nature. Human beings have always seen themselves as the center of the universe; all other living things are measured against humanity. But it can be humbling and enlightening to see ourselves as part of the natural world, and it can help us live in harmony with our surroundings instead of in conflict.

The human brain always wants to make order out of chaos—to make the unfamiliar familiar. This is why we imagine that animals are nothing more than oddly shaped people, with the same emotions and motivations as ourselves. Only by second-guessing this tendency, however, will we be able to fully appreciate the universe outside our own minds.

1. This passage primarily argues
    A. for anthropomorphism.
    B. against anthropomorphism.
    C. against interaction with wildlife.
    D. for living in harmony with nature.

2. Based on the main idea in this essay, which of the following would be unadvisable?
    A. the destruction of natural habitat to build a shopping center
    B. laws that make a distinction between animal rights and human rights
    C. a scientific trial to find out why jellyfish are sad
    D. a campaign to get homeless dogs and cats adopted

3. The author says that anthropomorphism is a natural result of our
    A. desire to make sense of things.
    B. will to destroy.
    C. confusion about ourselves.
    D. appreciation of the universe.

Exercise VI. Drawing on your knowledge of roots and words in context, read the following selection and define the italicized words. If you cannot figure out the meaning of the words on your own, look them up in a dictionary.

The *festal* organ composition is supposed to mark a day of rejoicing for the church. This year, however, the celebration was somewhat subdued. Members of the congregation are still mourning those lost in last autumn's disaster. By special arrangement, a solemn bell service was inserted into the middle of the musical piece. As the *plangent* tolling rang through the church, the tears of those gathered flowed freely.

UNIT SIX

SOMN
Latin SOMNUS, "sleep"

☰ *Can you think of another common word that comes from this root?*

SOMNOLENT   (säm´ nə lənt)   *adj.*   drowsy; sleepy
The already *somnolent* professor found that sitting through a slow afternoon of student presentations was agonizing.
syn: tired   *ant: alert*

SOPOR
Latin SOPOR, "sleep"

SOPORIFIC   (sop ər əf´ ək)   *adj.*   causing sleep or fatigue
L. *sopor* + *facere*, "to make" = *sleep-making*
Although we had been promised that the play would "astonish and amaze" us, we found the whole thing rather *soporific*.

SOPOR   (sō´ pər)   *n.*   sleep; drowsiness
Tim explained that his *sopor* was a result of the medicine given to him by the dentist, not a lack of interest.

LANG
Latin LANGUERE, "to be weak; to be faint"

LANGUID   (lan´ gwid)   *adj.*   lacking energy; weak
In response to James's voice, the sick dog was still able to give a *languid* wag of its tail.
syn: sluggish   *ant: active, lively*

LANGUISH   (lan´ gwish)   *v.*   to waste away
Bernard feared that if he was not granted parole, he would *languish* in prison for the rest of his life.
syn: weaken

☰ *It may seem that "language" should have some relation to these three words from* languere*, but it does not. The word* language *comes from the Latin* lingua*, "tongue."*

LANGUOR   (lan´ gər)   *n.*   a lack of physical or mental energy
The heat wave that the city had been experiencing for three weeks left residents in a state of *languor*.
syn: listlessness, lethargy

Angie's ANGER meets Larry's LANGUOR.

VIGIL
Latin VIGIL, "watchful"

VIGILANT (vi´ jə lənt) *adj.* on the alert; watchful
Having grown up in a tough neighborhood, Byron was known for keeping a *vigilant* eye on everything around him.
syn: aware *ant: inattentive*

VIGILANTE (vi jə lân´ tē) *n.* someone who takes law enforcement into his or her own hands
A number of mothers in the community decided that the police were not doing enough to combat teen violence, so they used *vigilante*-style tactics to clean up the neighborhood.

QUIES
Latin QUIESCERE, QUIETUS, "to rest"

ACQUIESCE (a kwē es´) *v.* to give in
L. *ad*, "toward" + *quiescere* = *to rest toward*
Geraldine finally *acquiesced* to the speaker's request to remain silent during the speech.
syn: submit, accede *ant: resist*

REQUIEM (re´ kwē əm) *n.* a song or religious service for the dead or lost
Verdi composed a moving *requiem* about Romeo and Juliet.
syn: elegy

QUITTANCE (kwi´ təns) *n.* a repayment; a compensation
After weeks of negotiation, the company finally allowed Jorge a *quittance* for his work.

▥ *The phrase "keeping a vigil" is connected to these vocabulary words. How?*

▥ *The first word of the Roman Catholic mass for the dead is* requies, *meaning "rest." A* requiem *can now mean any service or work intended to remember the departed.*

EXERCISES - UNIT SIX

Exercise I. Complete the sentence in a way that shows you understand the meaning of the italicized vocabulary word.

1.   Rather than *languishing* in his room during his mother's absence, the little boy…

2.   Lieutenant Eliot warned that if the soldiers were not *vigilant*, they might…

3.   The *sopor* into which Matthew drifted was a result of…

4.   Denise's *languid* pose suggested that she was feeling…

5.   In her *somnolent* state, Sandy should definitely not have been…

6.   The *languor* that settled over the farm was dispelled by…

7.   The lecturer's voice was exceedingly *soporific*, judging by…

8.   The head of the angry mob was once a sheriff, but he became a *vigilante* when…

9.   Trent would not *acquiesce* to his doctor's suggestion because…

10.   The jazz singer's mournful ballad was a fitting *requiem* for Michelle because…

11.   Many of the attorney's clients were businessman seeking a *quittance* from…

Exercise II. Fill in the blank with the best word from the choices below. One word will not be used.

acquiesce   vigilante   languor   soporific   languid

1.   Finding the magazine article _____, Kathleen fixed herself a cup of coffee and then finished reading.

2.   When the manager asked that I leave the store, I _____ only because I did not want to cause a scene.

3.   There seemed to be no escape from the _____ caused by Jaclyn's long illness.

4.   In response to the police officer's rapid-fire questions, the tired-looking boy gave a(n) _____ shrug.

Fill in the blank with the best word from the choices below. One word will not be used.

| requiem | vigilant | somnolent | quittance | sopor |

5. The insurance company granted Sam a _____ after his house was consumed by fire.

6. No amount of shouting could lift the children out of their television-induced _____.

7. Even the most superb gymnasts must be _____ for flaws in their own performance.

8. The _____ expression of the taxi driver made the passengers fear for their safety.

Fill in the blank with the best word from the choices below. One word will not be used.

| languish | vigilante | requiem | sopor |

9. When the regular army was destroyed, citizens gathered in _____ militias to protect their property.

10. Some critics have seen the actor's final film as a _____ for the bygone era of silent movies.

11. Without challenging and exciting subject material, the children will _____ in the classroom.

Exercise III. Choose the set of words that best completes the sentence.

1. The _____ effect of the drug made it difficult for Claude to remain _____ against mistakes in his work.
    A. languid; vigilant
    B. vigilant; somnolent
    C. languid; soporific
    D. soporific; vigilant

2. The unruly student was warned that if he did not _____ to the teacher's warnings, he would "_____ in this room with detentions until the end of the semester."
    A. languish; acquiesce
    B. acquiesce; languish
    C. acquiesce; sopor
    D. languish; vigilante

3. Sandra's already _____ mind was made sleepier by the _____ motion of the boat moving slowly through the water.
    A. vigilant; soporific
    B. soporific; vigilant
    C. somnolent; languid
    D. soporific; acquiescing

4.   While the _____ enforced strict and careful justice in Hodgeville, the uniformed police went about their tasks with a _____ that made them seem almost careless.
      A.   soporific; quittance
      B.   vigilantes; languor
      C.   languid; requiem
      D.   vigilantes; requiem

5.   Darren considered the pleasant _____ into which he now fell a fair _____ for weeks of backbreaking work.
      A.   requiem; quittance
      B.   vigilante; languor
      C.   languor; requiem
      D.   sopor; quittance

Exercise IV. Complete the sentence by inferring information about the italicized word from its context.

1.   If Franklin says that the music played by the radio station is *soporific*, he probably thinks that the station should…

2.   When the doctor sees that her patient is *languishing*, she may wonder if…

3.   Dana will probably not *acquiesce* to Patrick's demand for money if…

Exercise V. Fill in each blank with the word from the Unit that best completes the sentence, using the root we supply as a clue. Then, answer the questions that follow the paragraphs.

During World War II, the United States rounded up immigrants from Japan and American citizens of Japanese descent and kept them _____ (LANG) in internment camps for the duration of the war to avoid the possible threat of plots against American security. During World War II, Nazi Germany rounded up Jews and locked them up in camps, blaming them for the economic problems in the country after World War I. In the German camps, forced labor combined with starvation was only the slowest killer; the gas chambers, crematoria, and cruel forms of torture, including surgery without anesthesia, provided swifter death. Both societies chose a group of people based on ethnic backgrounds for confinement, and both societies were cruel to their captives—many Japanese had to wait as long as four years to return home, and, even though the government offered reparations for documented losses in 1948, many Japanese Americans received no payment from the government until the 1980s.

One major difference, though, is that because Adolf Hitler had enough support from his military and enough unquestioning support from the German people, he was not held accountable within his nation for his decisions, and there was no force to check him from putting his theories of racial purity into practice. President Roosevelt, in contrast, had an American public, weary from twelve years of the Great Depression, monitoring his actions, and his lease on power was up for renewal every four years. The insanity that was allowed to become official policy in Germany would have never passed the test of public approval, let alone the institutional roadblocks to executive action—the Congress and the Supreme Court.

Judging from these examples, what separates a republic from a dictatorship? Public _____ (VIGIL) does. Decision making is much more efficient for dictators: they face no angry voters (or voters of any kind), their strongmen can usually persuade individual dissidents to be quiet, and the press that dictators typically control can sway the opinions of society.

Augustus Caesar, the first Roman emperor, said that only nourishment and entertainment were necessary to keep a society sufficiently content to ignore the workings of the government. If there is a danger to American freedom, it is that our material wealth keeps us from noticing any news from the government that does not have to do with the economy. Because the average American does not keep any sort of surveillance on the environment, on industry regulation or deregulation, or on treaties with other nations, the government is not held accountable for many of its decisions. Therefore, any area in which the government is permitted to operate without accountability is one in which public apathy has allowed the American republic to become a semi-dictatorship.

1. Based on information in the passage, with which of the following would the author probably most agree?
   A. President Roosevelt was right to order the confinement of American citizens, even if they were of Japanese descent.
   B. A dictator has fewer obstacles to overcome in making decisions than the leader of a republic does.
   C. People tend to focus more on issues that affect society as a whole than on those that affect them individually.
   D. Congress played an important role in the internment of Japanese citizens.

2. In the author's opinion, what is the greatest threat to American freedom?
   A. internment based on ethnic background
   B. having elections only every four years
   C. the fact that the American press is permitted to operate freely
   D. the self-absorption with material possessions and entertainment

3. What was the difference between German and American treatment of ethnicity, according to the author?
   A. There was no difference; both Germans and Americans based decisions on race only.
   B. Hitler's decisions about ethnicity were created solely by economics.
   C. The treatment of Japanese Americans was based on security concerns.
   D. The treatment of Japanese citizens was based on Augustus Caesar's tactics.

Exercise VI. Drawing on your knowledge of roots and words in context, read the following selection and define the italicized words. If you cannot figure out the meaning of the words on your own, look them up in a dictionary. Note that *ambulat* means "walking."

Peace had finally settled over the orphanage. The *quiescent* halls of the younger children's ward satisfied the watchful eyes of the night nurse, whose duty it was to shepherd loitering or *somnambulating* children back to bed. Several weeks before, she had followed one such traveler all the way to the cafeteria, and watched in amusement as he seated himself at the table, waiting, in his sleep, for the meal to begin.

UNIT SEVEN

FORT
Latin FORTUITUS, "happening by chance"

FORTUITOUS (fôr tōō´ ə təs) *adj.* happening by a lucky accident or chance;
      fortunate
Although Kathleen was sorry that the lead clarinetist had fallen ill, she also saw
the event as *fortuitous* because it gave her a chance to exhibit her skills.
syn: providential   *ant: unlucky*

FORTUITY (fôr tōō´ ə tē) *n.* a chance or accident
By what *fortuity* did you come across the long-lost series of paintings?
syn: luck

AUSP
Latin AUSPEX, "bird-watcher; fortune-teller"

AUSPICES (aw´ spi səz) *n.* protection or support; patronage
The art director operated under the *auspices* of the Executive Vice President for
Creative Affairs.
syn: guidance

AUSPICIOUS (aw spi´ shəs) *adj.* followed by favorable circumstances
With the company boasting third-quarter gains of 15%, now is surely an
auspicious time to ask for a raise in your salary.
syn: propitious, promising

DEST
Latin DESTINARE, DESTINATUM, "to determine"

PREDESTINATION (prē des´ tin ā´ shən) *n.* the belief that one's fate has been
      determined in advance by a higher power
L. *pre,* "in advance" + *destinare* = decided in advance
Believers in *predestination* insisted that the bridge collapse was no accident.

DESTINE (des´ tin) *v.* to intend for a specific end or purpose
The latest children's film is *destined* to become one of the year's highest-grossing
pictures.

▥ *One important part of
ancient Roman religion
involved the prediction of
the future according to the
flight patterns of birds.
The person appointed to
interpret these patterns
was called the* auspex
(avis, *"bird," +* spex,
"watcher, seer").

▥ *Acting was always easy
for me. I don't believe in
predestination, but I do
believe that once you get
where ever it is you are
going, that is where you
were going to be.*
—Morgan Freeman,
American actor

SORT
Latin SORS, SORTIS, "chance, lot, fate"

CONSORTIUM   (con sôr´ shum)   *n.*   a group of companies or institutions
L. *con*, "together" + *sortis* = *having a common fate*
The university recently joined the Boston *consortium*, allowing students to enroll
in classes at any of its fourteen member schools.

CONSORT   (cən sōōrt´)   *v.*   1. to keep company; to associate
          (con´ sôrt)   *n.*   2. a companion, especially a romantic one
L. *con*, "together" + *sortis* = *common fate*
1. Sources report that the Mayor *consorts* with the local crime boss, as well as
   with other corrupt politicians.
2. Rumors began to spread about the actor and his new *consort*.

PROPIT
Latin PROPITIUS, "favorable"

PROPITIOUS   (prō pish´ əs)   *adj.*   lucky; favorable
The discovery of the new drug was *propitious*, coming, as it did, at the onset of a
deadly new virus.

PROPITIATE   (prō pish´ ē āt)   *v.*   to soothe or satisfy; to appease
Renee tried to *propitiate* her angry employers
by sending a letter of apology.
syn: reconcile

*The PRO PITCHER attempts to PROPITIATE
the baseball gods before the big game.*

▥ *Another name for
fortune-telling is
sortilege, meaning "the
reading of fate" (from
sors + legere, "to
read").*

▥ *A word that is related
to propitious is
serendipitous, which
means finding things of
value that were
unexpected. One
example is that of a
scientist who was trying
to find a new gas to use
in refrigerators and,
instead, came up with
Teflon. Serendipitous
comes to English
through a Persian fairy
tale called "The Three
Princes of Serendip."*

EXERCISES - UNIT SEVEN

Exercise I. Complete the sentence in a way that shows you understand the meaning of the italicized vocabulary word.

1. Deedee urged her brother not to *consort* with members of the rival team because…

2. The *fortuity* of Douglas's winning the football pool often made him wonder…

3. In order to *propitiate* the board of directors at Moransten Oil, Stanley…

4. The rangers viewed the return of endangered species to the park as an *auspicious* sign because…

5. Because Jin refused to acknowledge the possibility of *predestination*…

6. The captain and his first mate determined that the most *propitious* date to embark…

7. A *consortium* of oil-company executives was organized in order to…

8. Eric said that running into Adam had been *fortuitous* because…

9. Bert feared that his lack of math skills *destined* him to…

10. The artist was believed to be under the *auspices* of the wealthy Lopez family because…

Exercise II. Fill in the blank with the best word from the choices below. One word will not be used.

destine	fortuitous	propitiate	auspicious	consortium

1. The dean of students remarked upon how _____ it was that the distinguished professor should be in need of a job just when the college had a vacancy.

2. It seemed that no amount of flattery could _____ the demanding lord of the manor.

3. Henry wrongly believes that his past failures _____ him to a life of financial disaster.

4. We felt that the forest fire we encountered on the first day was not a(n) _____ indication of what we had in store.

Fill in the blank with the best word from the choices below. One word will not be used.

predestination   consortium   auspices   propitious

5.   Keisha's financial success is the result of her own hard work, not _____.

6.   As long as it operates under the _____ of its parent hospital, the clinic will continue to receive funding.

7.   Wendell wondered when the informal gathering of small business owners had become a powerful global _____ capable of making significant economic decisions.

Fill in the blank with the best word from the choices below. One word will not be used.

fortuity   propitious   predestination   consort

8.   The woman who had been the king's _____ would now become his queen.

9.   I felt it _____ that I had spotted the first robin of spring before anyone else had.

10.   Although the explorer insisted that he had triumphed through his own determination and intelligence, critics noted the _____ of his survival.

Exercise III. Choose the set of words that best completes the sentence.

1.   Richard was struck by the _____ of the company's success; many early economic indicators, he remembered, had not been _____.
   A.   consortium; fortuitous
   B.   fortuity; auspicious
   C.   auspices; fortuitous
   D.   consort; propitious

2.   Ancient priests believed that unless human beings _____ the gods, no divine being would _____ with mere mortals.
   A.   consorted; propitiate
   B.   propitiated; destine
   C.   propitiated; consort
   D.   consorted; destine

3.   A(n) _____ of music industry executives gathered under the _____ of the National Music Executives Association.
   A.   consortium; auspices
   B.   fortuity; consortium
   C.   auspice; consort
   D.   consortium; fortuity

4. Early American settlers believed that their fate was decided through _____, not random disasters or _____ occurrences.
    A. consort; auspicious
    B. predestination; fortuitous
    C. consortium; propitious
    D. auspices; fortuitous

5. New Year's is supposed to be an especially _____ time for starting a new job, but Chuck's new career was _____ to end in disaster.
    A. propitious; destined
    B. auspicious; consorted
    C. fortuitous; propitiated
    D. propitious; consorted

Exercise IV. Complete the sentence by inferring information about the italicized word from its context.

1. If the skier says it was *fortuitous* that he left the ski area when he did, we can infer that...

2. In order to *propitiate* their clients, attorneys at the firm of Jansen, Jansen, and Le Deux may...

3. If Andrea declares that she will not *consort* with the Michelsons, it is probably because she feels...

Exercise V. Fill in each blank with the word from the Unit that best completes the sentence, using the root we supply as a clue. Then, answer the questions that follow the paragraphs.

Have you looked at the dishwashing bubbles in your sink lately? Do you look at them as ways to tell how greasy your water is or as elements that could foretell your future? Tea leaves, cereal remnants, and ordinary playing cards might also have data for you if you take the time to look.

For those who practice divination (attempting to gain hidden knowledge magically or supernaturally), a variety of naturally occurring things can be employed to provide information about the present, past, and future. Forms of divination include palmistry, astrology, face reading, and phrenology. Many of these forms have significant historical backgrounds.

Palmistry, for example, may actually date to ancient times. In the fourth century BC, Aristotle mentioned palmistry in his writings; the early Romans, Hebrews, and Egyptians are all purported to have engaged in the study of lines in the hand and/or the shape of the hand.

Similarly, astrology has a long history in many parts of the world. The ancient Greeks developed astrological methods; in Arabia and Europe, astrology was widely known and practiced for thousands of years. The many divisions within astrology appear to provide something for anyone

who takes the time to investigate. Horary astrology, which deals with time, can provide information as to whether someone is _____ (DEST) to get a particular summer job. Those who read the daily horoscopes in the newspaper are drawing on information from sun sign astrology. If an individual is scheduled for elective surgery, medical astrology claims to have information regarding the most _____ (AUSP) day to have the surgery performed to avoid post-operative problems. Some Wall Street traders consult financial astrologers to make advantageous trading decisions and avoid financial misfortune.

Chaucer, Aristotle, and Hippocrates studied face reading; in China, skilled medical practitioners often used face reading to diagnose illnesses. Various facial features are said to be associated with personality characteristics and/or to hold information about the future. A shiny nose, for example, is said to reveal luck where money is concerned.

So, should we believe what astrology, palmistry, face reading, and other forms of fortune telling have to offer? Supporters of the use of divination procedures would argue affirmatively, pointing out the excellent track record and the long history associated with divination. They would tell us of their ability to predict wars and famines; they would remind us that influential people like Carl Jung saw value in astrology and other divinatory systems as ways of understanding how the mind works. They would advance the practice as a way to collect information regarding the future and not as a last resort to be tried when all else fails. They would also suggest that those who are lucky enough to realize its advantages also understand that there is no trickery involved; rather, divination allows information from the unconscious and often ignored portion of the human mind to be used in everyday situations.

1.   Based on the information in the essay, how might the author feel about Tarot cards or Ouija boards?
      A.   Tarot cards and Ouija boards should be used only by skilled professionals in divination.
      B.   Neither Tarot cards nor Ouija boards have an adequate historical base to support use in everyday situations.
      C.   The use of both Tarot cards and Ouija boards may be surrounded by skepticism regarding their capabilities to reveal the future.
      D.   Neither Tarot cards nor Ouija boards are significant forms of divination.

2.   The best title for the selection would be
      A.   Divination in Modern Times.
      B.   Fortune Telling and its Proponents.
      C.   Astrology.
      D.   The History of the Supernatural.

3.   According to the passage, which of the following statements is NOT true?
      A.   The unconscious mind is a repository for a great deal of knowledge and wisdom.
      B.   Divination is primarily associated with Western civilization.
      C.   Analysis of the shape of facial features can provide information on personality traits.
      D.   In many parts of the world, astrology has a long and respected history.

4.   The main idea of the selection is that
      A.   one should rely on one or more forms of divination to make day-to-day decisions.
      B.   one should use horoscopes, astrological signs, etc., to explain everyday happenings.
      C.   divination is relevant only for those who need to find ways to make life happier.
      D.   divination must be evaluated to determine what part it should play in our lives.

Exercise VI. Drawing on your knowledge of roots and words in context, read the following selection and define the italicized words. If you cannot figure out the meaning of the words on your own, look them up in a dictionary. Note that *as*, from *ad*, means "toward."

Gretchen expressed her belief in a kind of *fortuitism* when it came to evolutionary studies. In her examination of the gypsy moth, she found no clear link between any environmental factors and the adaptations that scientists had recorded. Rather, she likened the changes displayed by the moths to complicated *assortative* mating patterns. When the moths chose their mates, she believed, they did so based on the traits shared by each partner.

UNIT EIGHT

PORT
Latin PORTARE, PORTATUM, "to carry"

IMPORTUNE   (im pôr tōōn´)   v.   to urge or beg without end
Dennis promised to *importune* Congress until the ban on concealed weapons became law.
syn: plead

IMPORTUNATE   (im pôr´ chə nət)   *adj.*   extremely demanding; insistent
The baker finally surrendered and handed the *importunate* child a free cookie.

RAPPORT   (ra pôr´)   *n.*   a positive relationship
L. *re*, "back" + *ad*, "toward" + *portare* = *bringing back together*
When she was first hired, Wilma worked hard to establish a *rapport* with her fellow flight attendants.
syn: camaraderie, friendship

FER
Latin FERRE, "to bear; to carry"

INSUFFERABLE   (in su´ fər ə bəl)   *adj.*   impossible to bear; intolerable
Felicia found Robin *insufferable* and always tried to avoid her.

PREFERENTIAL   (pre fər ən´ shəl)   *adj.*   giving or showing an advantage to one over another
L. *pre*, "before" + *ferre* = *to carry before*
Many students in the class were angry over Ms. Bergman's *preferential* treatment of Sandra.

CONFERMENT   (kən fər´ mənt)   *n.*   the act of bestowing; a formal offer
L. *con*, "with" + *ferre* = *to bring with*
The *conferment* of power upon the new king did not take place without some disturbance in Parliament.

▥ *From the verb* portare *came the Latin word* portus, *meaning "harbor" ("that to which someone is brought"). Importune literally means "no harbor, no protection." Think of a boat without a harbor—it's open to all kinds of harassment by Mother Nature. Someone who* importunes *harasses in the same way, often at a time that is especially inconvenient or unsuitable for the person being bothered.*

▥ *To suffer (sub, "from beneath" and* ferre) *is to bear, as one would bear a burden. Someone insufferable (in = "not") cannot be endured.*

PHER, PHOR
Greek PHOREIN, "to carry; to bring"

PERIPHERY (pe ri´ fə rē) *n.* the outermost part or boundary
G. *peri*, "around" + *pherein* = *to carry around*
In ancient Rome, the dead were buried only on the *periphery* of the city.
syn: border, fringe   *ant: center*

EUPHORIA (ū fôr´ ē ə) *n.* a feeling of great happiness or well-being
G. *eu*, "good" + *pherein* = *bringing good*
Following his victory at the Milvian Bridge, Constantine was filled with a deep feeling of *euphoria*.
syn: joy   *ant: misery*

GEST
Latin GERERE, GESTUM, "to bear; to carry"

CONGESTED (kun jest´ əd) *adj.* overcrowded; too tightly packed
L. *con*, "together" + *gestum* = *carried together*
It can often take hours to get home during rush hour because of the *congested* highways.
syn: blocked, full   *ant: clear, empty*

GESTATE (jes´ tāt) *v.* to conceive and develop in the mind or body
My teacher always told me to give myself plenty of time for ideas to *gestate*.

GESTICULATE (jes ti´ kū lāt) *v.* to make gestures for emphasis
As the man gave us the complicated instructions, he *gesticulated* in a lively fashion.

The GESTICULATING JESTER made insulting GESTURES.

▥ *Your* peripheral *vision refers to what you can see to the side while looking straight ahead. This type of vision is extremely important when driving.*

▥ *A pheromone (phorein + hormone) is a chemical that is emitted by a living creature and carried through water or air to other members of that creature's species, usually as a means of attracting a mate.*

EXERCISES - UNIT EIGHT

Exercise I. Complete the sentence in a way that shows you understand the meaning of the italicized vocabulary word.

1.   The patient's arteries were heavily *congested* because…

2.   The *rapport* between the cabaret singer and her pianist was the result of…

3.   Isabel often felt she was on the *periphery* of her family's life rather than…

4.   Many of my classmates found the new student in our history class *insufferable* because…

5.   Professor Connor barely *gesticulated* at all during the long lecture, which made…

6.   The *conferment* of honors upon Walter resulted in…

7.   Cal was so *importunate* in his pursuit of powerful allies and friends that…

8.   The *euphoria* Raymond experienced when he saw Tina was like…

9.   When Greg *importuned* the city for looser parking regulations…

10. Terence received *preferential* treatment…

11. The architect often needed time for his ideas to *gestate* because…

Exercise II. Fill in the blank with the best word from the choices below. One word will not be used.

euphoria   importunate   conferment   insufferable   gestate

1.   The _____ of gifts and respect upon the ruler of the tiny country lasted only until he was removed from power.

2.   The _____ patient was not satisfied even after he had the opinions of two highly respected surgeons.

3.   Once the proposal has _____ for several months in the minds of council members, we can bring it forth for discussion.

4.   "There is nothing more _____," warned my mother, "than people who talk only about themselves."

Fill in the blank with the best word from the choices below. One word will not be used.

congested   importune   periphery   preferential   euphoria

5.   Because of his connection to the hospital, Milt received _____ care even when other patients were waiting.

6.   Since she was supplied with all the funds she needed, the opera star saw no need to _____ her manager for additional support.

7.   Although Vance tried to be gracious to the losing team, he could hardly hide his _____ at winning the championship.

8.   Rivers _____ with leaves and debris made the kayaker's journey all the more difficult.

Fill in the blank with the best word from the choices below. One word will not be used.

periphery   gesticulate   rapport   congested

9.   Jill tried to focus on the parts of the dream that she remembered, but they remained on the _____ of her waking mind.

10. Because Nanette did not ever _____ or raise her voice, she got a reputation for being an unemotional person.

11. The growing lack of _____ between members of the soccer team seemed certain to result in a big argument.

Exercise III. Choose the set of words that best completes the sentence.

1.   Pilar was so _____ in her demands for a larger salary that her boss began to find her _____.
     A. importunate; insufferable
     B. preferential; importunate
     C. congested; insufferable
     D. importunate; preferential

2.   Because Caitlyn had developed a(n) _____ with several of the servers at the restaurant, she always got _____ treatment there.
     A. euphoria; insufferable
     B. rapport; preferential
     C. conferment; importunate
     D. periphery; preferential

3.   Marcia _____ wildly as she gave her victory speech, revealing her total _____.
      A.   gestated; rapport
      B.   gesticulated; euphoria
      C.   importuned; conferment
      D.   importuned; euphoria

4.   Though citizens had repeatedly _____ the Department of Transportation for a better traffic system in the downtown area, its agenda was so _____ that the topic was never brought up.
      A.   importuned; congested
      B.   gestated; importunate
      C.   gesticulated; insufferable
      D.   importuned; preferential

5.   Though Adam did not actively consider Anita's request to lend her money, he allowed it to _____ on the _____ of his mind.
      A.   importune; conferment
      B.   gesticulate; euphoria
      C.   gestate; periphery
      D.   gestate; conferment

Exercise IV. Complete the sentence by inferring information about the italicized word from its context.

1.   The *conferment* of honors upon Esther will probably make her feel…

2.   The leaders of the small colony are probably *importunate* in asking for their independence because…

3.   If Kathy and Don choose to stand on the *periphery* of the crowd, it may be because…

Exercise V. Fill in each blank with the word from the Unit that best completes the sentence, using the root we supply as a clue. Then, answer the questions that follow the paragraphs.

There's an invisible epidemic plaguing our college campuses that can't be cured by antibiotics or anti-inflammatories. It is an epidemic of sexual assault against women, and researchers warn that it is on the rise. Few of the nation's colleges, though, are taking appropriate action in reporting rape and sexual assault.

The US Department of Education's Office of Post-Secondary Education found that 23% of women experience some type of sexual offense while attending college. Some colleges have responded by pouring money into rape-prevention programs and hiring extra security officers. One thing most colleges haven't done, however, is change the way they report these crimes for statistical purposes.

Researchers at the University of Cincinnati recently found that only slightly more than a third of schools are complying with the Clery Act, a law that mandates filing annual crime reports with the Department of Education to tally offenses like rapes and sexual assaults. The majority of colleges and universities are generating reports that don't contain the specific information required by the law. The study also found there is no standard definition for sexual assaults and rapes among the schools, that fewer than half the institutions provide new students with sexual-assault awareness education, and that only 38% require campus police officers to undergo sexual-assault sensitivity training. These trends are changing, but too slowly.

The study's results buttressed some advocacy groups' complaints that universities are hiding campus crimes, especially those of a sexual nature, to make the schools seem more _____ (FER) to prospective students. Lawmakers contend that this practice is misleading, especially to students looking for a safe setting in which to attend classes.

"Universities want you to think their campuses are like mom and apple pie, but students are getting raped...and we don't know about it," Representative Howard McKeon, a Republican from California, told the *Sacramento Bee* newspaper. Consumers should be able to rely on colleges to provide an accurate picture of security on their campuses, the congressman added.

One student, a sophomore at the University of California at Santa Barbara, was looking to switch schools after she was sexually assaulted at a house party on the _____ (PHER) of that campus in 1999. She checked the US Department of Education's website listing crime statistics for all of the University of California's campuses to find the safest one. She found a line of zeros next to the UC Davis's listings for rapes and attempted rapes and enrolled the next month.

Shortly after she arrived on campus, however, the student learned that those comforting zeros were misleading. "The first friend I made had been raped in her dorm room, but it never appeared in those numbers," she told the newspaper; since then, she has used her personal story to _____ (PORT) University of California officials to sanction administrators for underreporting sexual crimes on their campuses.

1. Which statement best summarizes the main idea of this passage?
   A. Sexual assaults on campuses are rising.
   B. College administrators are concerned about security on their campuses.
   C. Colleges are not accurately reporting sexual assault cases.
   D. Colleges are trying to protect their reputations in a highly competitive environment.

2. The author of this passage claims that
   A. colleges should accurately report statistics on sexually related crimes.
   B. failure of schools to meet the requirement of the Clery Act is a minor violation.
   C. cases of sexual harassment are rising on college campuses.
   D. students have no right to rely on colleges for an accurate assessment of campus security.

3. The Clery Act requires colleges to
   A. keep records of all campus crime.
   B. file a report with the federal government that breaks down certain offenses.
   C. make sure campus security officers handle sexually related crimes properly.
   D. provide rape-prevention classes.

4. Which title best fits this passage?
   A. Sexual Harassment: The Invisible Epidemic
   B. Clery Act Gets No Respect from Colleges
   C. One Student's Nightmare
   D. Colleges Keep Crime in the Shadows

Exercise VI. Drawing on your knowledge of roots and words in context, read the following selection and define the italicized words. If you cannot figure out the meaning of the words on your own, look them up in a dictionary. Note that *dia* means "through" and *a*, from *ad*, means "toward."

In an attempt to discover the cause of the patient's baffling condition, doctors reviewed the strange array of symptoms. The patient was often short of breath and suffered from *diaphoresis*. Fluid loss from such perspiration should have resulted in dehydration, but instead, the body seemed to have sufficient or excessive water levels. In addition, the *afferent* nerves seemed to be malfunctioning; impulses that should have traveled inward to the brain were halted, and the patient's sensations were compromised.

UNIT NINE

SOL
Latin SOLUS, "alone"

SOLIPSISM   (so´ lip sizm)   *n.*   the theory that the self is the only reality; self-absorption
L. *solus* + *ipse*, "self" = *the self alone*
What some theater critics called the actress's "refreshing sense of her own presence" others called "overwhelming *solipsism*."

DESOLATE   (des´ ə lət)   *adj.*   deserted and lonely
L. *de*, "from" + *solus* = *alone from*
When Lupe saw the *desolate* midnight street, she felt a shiver of sadness.
syn: *bare*   ant: *crowded, lively*

SOLILOQUY   (sə lil´ ə kwē)   *n.*   a literary or dramatic speech spoken by a solitary character
L. *solus* + *loqui*, "to speak" = *to speak alone*
The *soliloquy* captures the turmoil of the young prince's mind as he contemplates life and death.
syn: *monologue*   ant: *dialogue, conversation*

MONO
Greek MONOS, "one"

MONOTONOUS   (mə not´ ə nəs)   *adj.*   unvarying; lacking in variety
G. *monos* + *tonos*, "tone" = *one tone*
Ruben said that he found meetings *monotonous* and rarely cared about what was said during them.
syn: *boring*   ant: *varying*

MONOSYLLABIC   (mo nō si la´ bik)   *adj.*   having only one syllable
G. *monos* + *sullabe*, "syllable" = *having one syllable*
Jake was considered an antisocial guy because he avoided eye contact and made only *monosyllabic* statements, if any.
                         ant: *polysyllabic*

MONOTONE   (mo´ nə tōn)   *n.*   a sameness of sound, style, manner, or color
G. *monos*, "one" + *tonos*, "tone, sound" = *one tone; one sound*
The conductor's dreary *monotone* went on announcing stops as the crowd milled around on the platform.

Probably the most famous soliloquy in English is spoken by Hamlet while he is contemplating the meaning of his own life. It begins with six very simple monosyllabic words of only two or three letters, yet it poses an essential human question that applies to all people: "To be or not to be…"

I feel monotony and death to be almost the same. —Charlotte Brontë

VULG
Latin VULGUS, "crowd"

DIVULGE   (də vulgʹ)   *v.*   to make public
L. *dis*, "among" + *vulgus* = *to spread among the crowd*
Government officials are refusing to *divulge* the reasons for the cabinet member's resignation.

VULGAR   (vulʹ gər)   *adj.*   of the common people
Throughout the medieval period, *vulgar* Latin was the most widely known language on the planet.

POLY, POLL
Greek POLUS, "many"

POLYMATH   (poʹ lē math)   *n.*   a person with knowledge of many subjects
G. *polus* + *manthanein*, "to learn" = *learned in many things*
Leonardo da Vinci was a *polymath* with extensive knowledge of literature, art, and science.

HOI POLLOI   (hoy pə loyʹ)   *n.*   the common people; the masses
The chef sniffed snobbishly, "My dishes were not intended for the *hoi polloi*."

POLYGLOT   (poʹ lē glot)   *n.*   a person with a knowledge of several languages
G. *polus* + *glotta*, "tongue" = *many tongues*
The new chair of the foreign language department was a *polygot* who spoke French, wrote books in Spanish, watched Italian films, and taught class in Greek.

POLLY the POLYGLOT parrot squawks in three languages.

The fourth-century scholar St. Jerome is credited for translating the Old and New Testaments into Latin. Because his translation was intended to make the Bible accessible to the general masses of people instead of just to the clergy, it is called the Vulgate.

Like the in English and la in French or Spanish, hoi is an article meaning "the." Hoi polloi comes straight from the Greek and means "the many."

EXERCISES - UNIT NINE

Exercise I. Complete the sentence in a way that shows you understand the meaning of the italicized vocabulary word.

1.   The soldiers were warned not to *divulge* the battle plans because...

2.   The old elementary school playground had been *desolate* since...

3.   Because Katie both sang and spoke in a *monotone*, she was encouraged to...

4.   Fritz declared that the song was appropriate for the *hoi polloi* rather than...

5.   Because Lloyd's conversational style was *monosyllabic*, he earned a reputation as...

6.   Many in the audience felt that the Presidential Debate turned into a *soliloquy* when...

7.   Because they considered Neil a *polymath*, his friends often...

8.   The sports critic called bullfighting "the ideal *vulgar* pastime" because...

9.   When Edgar explained that he was a *polyglot* as a result of his upbringing, we knew he had...

10.   We could tell that Danielle had fully embraced the idea of *solipsism* when she...

11.   When Calvin's daily exercise routine started to become *monotonous*,...

Exercise II. Fill in the blank with the best word from the choices below. One word will not be used.

polymath	desolate	solipsism	monosyllabic	soliloquy

1.   Nell's _____ made the people she encountered wonder if she noticed them at all.

2.   Ruby's _____ replies to my questions let me know she did not feel like talking.

3.   Despite a moving _____ about the sinfulness of violence, the hero of the novel makes up his mind to kill his brother.

4.   Dorothy studied nonstop in the hopes of being like the _____ she most admired.

Fill in the blank with the best word from the choices below. One word will not be used.

soliloquy　　　monotone　　　desolate　　　monotonous

5.　The speech teacher reminded his students to vary their pitch rather than speaking in a
＿＿＿＿＿＿＿＿＿＿.

6.　All the New Year's Eve partiers went home to sleep, and the streets seemed empty and
＿＿＿＿＿＿＿＿＿＿.

7.　Finding the endless repetition of the same popular music rather ＿＿＿＿＿＿＿＿＿＿, the pianist
decided to try some experimentation.

Fill in the blank with the best word from the choices below. One word will not be used.

divulge　　　polymath　　　polyglot　　　vulgar　　　hoi polloi

8.　The poet disdained anyone who stooped to write in the ＿＿＿＿＿＿＿＿＿＿ tongue.

9.　A ＿＿＿＿＿＿＿＿＿＿ by training, inspector Morrison was able to converse in any of six different
languages.

10.　Chef Mingus swore that he would never ＿＿＿＿＿＿＿＿＿＿ the secret to his award-winning
turkey pie.

11.　Jacob pointed out to the arrogant banker that members of the so-called ＿＿＿＿＿＿＿＿＿＿ made
up a majority of the bank's loan customers.

Exercise III. Choose the set of words that best completes the sentence.

1.　The ＿＿＿＿ repetition of low shrubs and concrete buildings, unbroken by any hint of life or activity, told
us immediately that this was a ＿＿＿＿ place.
　A.　vulgar; monosyllabic
　B.　monotonous; desolate
　C.　monosyllabic; vulgar
　D.　desolate; vulgar

2.　The wealthy, self-centered businessman's ＿＿＿＿ was so extreme that he acknowledged the existence of the
＿＿＿＿ only to bolster his view of himself.
　A.　hoi polloi; polymaths
　B.　soliloquy; polyglots
　C.　monotone; solipsism
　D.　solipsism; hoi polloi

3.   Because he delivered the entire _____ in a mumbled _____, the actor earned the criticism of both the audience and the other cast members.
     A.   soliloquy; monotone
     B.   polymath; solipsism
     C.   soliloquy; solipsism
     D.   monotone; polyglot

4.   Ancient scholars did not consider someone a _____ just because he or she could speak fluently in one of the _____ tongues.
     A.   polymath; monotonous
     B.   soliloquy; monosyllabic
     C.   polyglot; vulgar
     D.   monotone; desolate

5.   Alice, a _____ with an appetite for all kinds of learning and conversation, never limited herself to _____ statements.
     A.   polymath; monosyllabic
     B.   monotone; vulgar
     C.   polyglot; desolate
     D.   solipsism; vulgar

Exercise IV. Complete the sentence by inferring information about the italicized word from its context.

1.   Because Kenneth will not *divulge* the location of his car, we can assume he...

2.   If Arthur finds the decorating scheme *monotonous*, he may suggest that...

3.   To back up her claim that she is a *polymath*, Rebecca may do things like...

Exercise V. Fill in each blank with the word from the Unit that best completes the sentence, using the root we supply as a clue. Then, answer the questions that follow the paragraphs.

The Nevada desert was transformed in the 1950s by the emergence of Las Vegas as the gambling and entertainment mecca of America. The arid and _____ (SOL) expanse blossomed into one of the most entertaining tourist destinations the world has ever known. On any given day or night, you can find the _____ (POLL) rubbing elbows with the wealthiest high rollers. The lights never go out. If you want to forget time, this is the place for you because there are no clocks to be seen inside the casinos—one must not _____ (VULG) the time to the gambler who has won $10,000 and is on his third carafe of coffee. The _____ (MONO) beeps or mechanical swoosh of the levers on the slot machines rhythmically chant their hopeful pitch to the gambler, interrupted only by the clatter of quarters cascading into the tray.

Everything is provided! You can get a buffet dinner for under $10—roast beef and all the trimmings if that is your heart's desire. You can catch a wonderful show at a very reasonable price. Top-name entertainers star in Las Vegas regularly, and some, past their prime but lucky, are permanent fixtures at the more famous casinos. Everything is larger than life and designed to make your experience the same. You can see pirates capture a frigate or hear huge white tigers purr. You can see has-beens in sequins. From the sublime to the ridiculous, all is there for your pleasure and entertainment. It is wonderful and wondrous! Isn't that what entertainment should be?

If you have never gone to Las Vegas, you need to put it on your list. Who knows? You may be the one to beat the astronomical odds and win a million dollars. Even if you don't, you are guaranteed to be entertained, to see splendor, tasteless and tasteful beauty beyond your wildest dreams, and to witness productions to take your breath away. Come to the city that grew out of the arid desert into one of the entertainment capitals of the world!

1. Why are there no clocks in the Las Vegas casinos?
    A. Clocks are real; the Vegas experience is surreal.
    B. Clocks are a distraction, and gamblers mustn't be reminded about time.
    C. Clocks would take the fun out of winning.
    D. Clocks reinforce the passing of time and pleasure.

2. What is the greatest accomplishment of Las Vegas, according to the author?
    A. "Top-name entertainers" perform in many of the famous casinos.
    B. It has become the "entertainment capital" of America.
    C. You can "win a million dollars" in the casinos.
    D. It "grew out of the arid desert" to become a city for gambling.

3. The tone of this essay is
    A. informative.
    B. sarcastic.
    C. straightforward.
    D. persuasive.

Exercise VI. Drawing on your knowledge of roots and words in context, read the following selection and define the italicized words. If you cannot figure out the meaning of the words on your own, look them up in a dictionary. Note that *mania* means "enthusiasm" and *onymous* means "named."

Sean does not recall exactly when he went from being an ordinary employee with above-average dedication to his job to a workaholic who spends every spare moment of his time at the office. Chances are, though, that this *monomania* developed as the result of a terribly unhappy love affair that ended a year ago. In an attempt to fill the void, Sean started Sean's Computer Solutions, a.k.a. Computer Carnival (legally abbreviated as SeanComp, Inc). Spending all of his time at this *polyonymous* business helps Sean focus on something other than the pain in his life.

UNIT TEN

TOT
Latin TOTUS, "whole"

TOTALITARIAN (tō ta lə târ´ ē ən) *adj.* having to do with a government in which one person, group, or party controls everything
The new ruler was gaining power so quickly that people feared he would establish a *totalitarian* state.

TOTALITY (tō ta´ lə tē) *n.* completeness
The *totality* of Hank's financial loss did not hit him until his home was repossessed.
syn: whole

HOL
Greek HOLOS, "whole"

HOLISTIC (hō lis´ tək) *adj.* concerning the whole rather than the parts
After years of specializing only in bone diseases, Dr. Russo decided to become a more *holistic* practitioner and began to attend classes in nutrition and exercise.

CATHOLIC (kath´ lək) *adj.* covering a broad range; universal
G. *kata*, "according to" + *holos* = *according to the whole*
The New York Times has a *catholic* appeal; men and women of all ages, races, and ethnicities read it.

ant: narrow

SUM
Latin SUMMUS, "highest; most"

CONSUMMATE (kân´ səm ət) *adj.* perfect or ideal, especially in skill or accomplishment
L. *con*, intensifier, + *summus* = *the highest; most finished; perfected*
Over the years, my mother's *consummate* graciousness impressed hundreds of visitors to our home.

SUMMATION (sum ā´ shən) *n.* an accumulation; a total result
The report given by Doctor Mikowski was the *summation* of four years of research.

Sidebar notes

▥ *Look at all the words associated with a* totalitarian *form of government:* dictatorship, tyrannical, autocratic, fascistic, authoritarian, despotic, oppressive, *and* undemocratic.

▥ *To* consummate *is "to finish." A French soup that uses up or finishes off leftovers is called a* consommé.

TRUNC, TRENC
Latin TRUNCARE, TRUNCATUM, "to cut"

TRENCHANT   (tren´chənt)   *adj.*   sharply effective or insightful
Despite the speaker's *trenchant* arguments for tax reform, the crowd voted against his proposal.
syn: clear

TRUNCATE   (trun´kāt)   *v.*   to cut short in the middle
Because the actress ran out of time, she was forced to *truncate* her acceptance speech.
syn: curtail   *ant: expand, prolong*

PART
Latin PARS, PARTIS, "part"

PARCEL   (pär´səl)   *v.*   to divide into parts and distribute
The baker *parceled* out the cookies among his seventeen children.

PARSE   (pärs)   *v.*   to examine or analyze
The English professor urged the students to *parse* each sentence in the sonnet in order to get a better understanding of the meaning.

REPARTEE   (re pär tā´)   *n.*   a quick, witty conversation
Swift *repartee* between members of the close family gives us some idea of the relaxed cheerfulness they feel around one another.
syn: banter

Witty REPARTEE makes a party a PART-TAY!

Ⅲ *Based on their Latin origins, how are* trenchant *and* truncate *related?*

Ⅲ *The French word for "leave, depart" is* partir. Repartee *literally means "departing again" and refers to an exchange in which speakers frequently depart from the subject to make witty remarks.*

EXERCISES - UNIT TEN

Exercise I. Complete the sentence in a way that shows you understand the meaning of the italicized vocabulary word.

1. Our fears that the new administration would install a *totalitarian* government came true when...

2. Because Rick's message about the party was *truncated*, it was difficult for us to...

3. As part of his *holistic* approach to education, Professor Jordan stressed...

4. The *summation* of all the volunteers' efforts to provide adequate medical care to the children of the town was...

5. *Repartee* between Juggles the Clown and his sidekick, Eddie, usually...

6. The importance of civil rights is *catholic* rather than...

7. Analysts are finding it difficult to *parse* the economic forecast because...

8. Many critics considered Fiona a *consummate* actress because...

9. The city decided to *parcel* out the land on the edge of town rather than...

10. Mike's *trenchant* comments on the use of the trumpet in modern jazz compositions made the other musicians...

11. The *totality* of the ruin caused by the tornado amazed us because...

Exercise II. Fill in the blank with the best word from the choices below. One word will not be used.

totality	holistic	totalitarian	trenchant

1. Stephanie strove for a _____ rule over the other children rather than a democratic relationship.

2. The _____ of the ruler's domination was a result of years of brutal crackdowns.

3. The film lacks a certain _____ quality that could have tied it all together.

Fill in the blank with the best word from the choices below. One word will not be used.

catholic	repartee	consummate	truncate	parcel

4. Maureen was a reader of _____ tastes, picking up whatever the library had to offer.

5. Maria and her sisters often engaged in witty _____ about who was the best athlete.

6. Bethany must now choose whether she will _____ out her winnings among friends and family or let the money accrue interest in the bank.

7. Our neighbor's _____ grilling techniques made him a popular "guest chef" at our barbecues.

Fill in the blank with the best word from the choices below. One word will not be used.

repartee	summation	parse ·	truncate	trenchant

8. Connie was able to _____ the difficult poem with little trouble because she was familiar with the author's other works.

9. The artist told his supporters that the huge mural was not the work of one person alone, but the _____ of many people's time and concern.

10. Linda was praised for her _____ essay on the current political situation in France.

11. Shondra's science presentation was _____ because of a sudden power outage.

Exercise III. Choose the set of words that best completes the sentence.

1. Freddie's _____ journalistic skills ensured that his readers got a _____, insightful article in every Sunday paper.
    A. totalitarian; catholic
    B. consummate; trenchant
    C. holistic; catholic
    D. trenchant; holistic

2. During the final exam, a _____ of the year's work, students were asked to _____ a lengthy essay for meaning.
    A. repartee; parse
    B. totalitarian; parcel
    C. repartee; truncate
    D. summation; parse

3.   The _____ of the poet's work surprised many critics, who had assumed that the body of poems had been _____ by the poet's early death.
      A.   totality; truncated
      B.   summation; parceled
      C.   repartee; parsed
      D.   totality; parsed

4.   Though the scientists once believed that the human brain _____ out different functions to different areas, they now support a more _____ view of its performance.
      A.   truncated; consummate
      B.   parsed; trenchant
      C.   parceled; holistic
      D.   parsed; totalitarian

5.   The politician kept up a humorous _____ with the citizens he represented, but also tried to stick to subjects of _____ significance.
      A.   repartee; trenchant
      B.   summation; holistic
      C.   totality; consummate
      D.   repartee; catholic

Exercise IV. Complete the sentence by inferring information about the italicized word from its context.

1.   If Ivan's arguments in favor of free speech are *trenchant* enough, the people listening to him will probably...

2.   *Repartee* between baseball players on opposing teams may be seen by some fans as...

3.   Because many musicians consider Hal a *consummate* pianist, they will probably suggest that he...

Exercise V. Fill in each blank with the word from the Unit that best completes the sentence, using the root we supply as a clue. Then, answer the questions that follow the paragraphs.

Government has been an established institution from the inception of society, and it serves to define and enforce rules of conduct for members of a group, especially that conduct which affects the group as a whole. In the United States, the idea of political freedom—that every human being possesses equal rights and is, by nature, born free—underpins the formation and foundation of our government. In our society, government exists to protect those rights, ensuring that stronger individuals do not violate the rights of the weaker. In addition, because the United States was founded on the idea of human equality, our government rules through the consent of the people.

According to these ideals, then, the existence of a _____ (TOT) government is morally wrong.

Under such a government, rule is based on subordination of the individual to the state. The state has absolute control over people's lives, making individuals servants of the state and prohibiting freedom of choice or expression. Often, such a government is ruled by one party or one leader, who uses terror tactics to maintain control. These governments may rely on secret police, censorship, religious intolerance, and economic monopoly to suppress individual expression.

One concept integral to the existence of the government is expressed in _____ (TRENC) fashion by the Declaration of Independence: the people's right to demand change. The populace cannot be expected to submit to tyranny, according to the Declaration. The people have not only moral right, but also moral obligation to overthrow a government that acts to destroy the natural rights of human beings. Because a dictatorship makes the good of the state the _____ (TOT) of individuals' existence, it destroys the integrity of the individual, and in doing so, it renders itself invalid.

1.   What is the purpose of government, according to the passage?
      A. to protect the rights of people
      B. to keep people safe
      C. to enforce rules of conduct for society
      D. to make laws

2.   What is the main argument that the article presents against totalitarian government?
      A. It is not based on the consent of individuals.
      B. It violates fundamental human rights.
      C. It uses terror tactics to control people.
      D. Totalitarian regimes often have only one ruler.

3.   With which of the following, judging by the passage, would the founders of the government agree?
      A. The human spirit naturally rebels against oppression.
      B. People need church and family.
      C. Dictators are not strong enough.
      D. The laws are illegal.

4.   What is the main idea of the last paragraph?
      A. The United States rule of law is the best way to govern a population.
      B. Under totalitarian rule, all individuals are completely subordinate to the State.
      C. Totalitarian governments can completely suppress any citizen's liberties.
      D. The sentiments in the Declaration of Independence oppose totalitarianism.

Exercise VI. Drawing on your knowledge of roots and words in context, read the following selection and define the italicized words. If you cannot figure out the meaning of the words on your own, look them up in a dictionary. Note that *bi* means "two" and *andric* means "male."

The insect has a *bipartite* body structure neatly suited to grasping and ingesting food and making a quick escape from predators. Either part of the body can serve as the "head" because the organism is entirely covered with sensory receptors that act as eyes, ears, and nose. One of the most interesting features of this organism is its *holandric* traits. Males of the species may develop an extra antenna during the larval stage, while females consistently have two antennae.

UNIT ELEVEN

SER
Latin SERERE, SERTUM, "to join"

> ▥ Series *is another word that we get from* serere; *it means "a group of things joined together."*

ASSERTION (ə sûr´ shən) *n.* something declared or stated positively
L. *ad*, "toward, to" + *sertum* = *to join to*
Lennie's *assertion* that he was a creative genius prompted shouts of disagreement from the crowd.

EXERTION (ek zûr´ shən) *n.* the use of power and strength
L. *ex*, "out of" + *sertum* = *to join out; to stretch out*
Chloe's swim across the lake required so much *exertion* that she was exhausted afterward.
>   *ant: relaxation*

DISSERTATION (di sər tā´ shən) *n.* a formal and long paper, written for a
    degree at a university or college
L. *dis*, "apart" + *sertum* = *to join things that are apart; to discuss*
Marietta's *dissertation* was entitled "The Sleep-Inducing Effects of Clock Ticking."

CERT
Latin CERNERE, CERTUM, "to separate; to distinguish; to decide"

> ▥ *The word* concert *describes the harmonious condition achieved after an agreement is decided* (certum) *upon. To* disconcert (dis, *"not"* + concert) *is to upset this harmony.*

DISCONCERT (dis kən sûrt´) *v.*   1. to upset and confuse
                                 adj. 2. bothered; concerned
                                           (*disconcerted; disconcerting*)
1. Marc didn't mean to *disconcert* his parents when he wasn't home by curfew; he had just lost track of time.
2. The thought of Nadia becoming class president was *disconcerting* to her fellow classmates, who felt she was unorganized and incompetent.

CERTITUDE (sər´ tə tōōd) *n.* a certainty; an inevitability
Winnie expressed *certitude* that her train would reach the station in time.
syn: surety   *ant: doubt*

ASCERTAIN (a sər tān´) *v.* to discover;
    to find out
L. *ad*, "to" + *cernere* = *to determine*
The lack of evidence made it difficult to *ascertain* the precise angle of the gunshot.
syn: determine

Warning! ASCERTAIN the TERRAIN before skiing down the hill.

NEX

Latin NECTERE, NEXUS, "to connect; to bind"

ANNEX   (ə neks´)   *v.*   to attach oneself; to take over
L. *ad*, "to" + *nexus = to bind to (oneself)*
The city of Smyrna sought to *annex* land from a neighboring town, but the state legislature denied the motion.

ant: disconnect

NEXUS   (nek´ səs)   *n.*   the core or center; a connection
The restaurant was located at the *nexus* of the town's two busiest streets.
syn: crux   *ant: periphery*

LIG, LIA

Latin LIGARE, LIGATUM, "to bind"

LIAISON   (lē ā´ zän)   *n.*   an intermediary; a go-between
Sheila had an interview the other day for a position as a White House press *liaison*.

OBLIGATORY   (ə blig´ ə tôr ē)   *adj.*   expected or required
L. *ob*, "upon" + *ligare = to bind upon*
Although Rachel had never been a big fan of the coach, she offered him the *obligatory* handshake when he retired.
syn: mandatory

LIGATURE   (lig´ ə tchər)   *n.*   a binding or joining
When the rope that held the bundle snapped, Jay had to improvise by using his belt as a *ligature*.

Although liaison *may look a bit different from words like* obligatory *and* ligature, *it is related to them. Just remember that the "g" of* ligare *dropped out when the word came into French.*

To oblige is literally to bind someone to you through contracts or promises, so that the person owes you something; something obligatory is owed, even if you don't want to give it.

EXERCISES - UNIT ELEVEN

Exercise I. Complete the sentence in a way that shows you understand the meaning of the italicized vocabulary word.

1. Fran's *assertion* that she grew the juiciest tomatoes prompted her friends to...

2. In order to *ascertain* the value of the newly discovered gem, its owner...

3. Geraldine said that the *obligatory* congratulations offered by her mother-in-law were...

4. During one of her research experiments, the marine biologist was *disconcerted* to find that...

5. The physical *exertion* required to lift the box was so great that...

6. A *ligature* between the boats allowed the captain to...

7. In an attempt to *annex* several smaller companies, Newton Refrigerator Corporation...

8. At the *nexus* of the two communities...

9. Hallie was chosen to act as a *liaison* between her two best friends because...

10. Bob's *dissertation* on the nesting habits of migrating swans...

11. We can say with *certitude* that no one has been in the house because...

Exercise II. Fill in the blank with the best word from the choices below. One word will not be used.

nexus	ascertain	liaison	dissertation	assertion

1. The union members nominated an official to serve as a(n) _____ between the union and employers.

2. Claire said that she wanted only a short summary of the book, not a(n) _____ on it.

3. At the _____ of his book on evolution is the belief that birds did not come from dinosaurs.

4. Because the fire had badly damaged the computer system, we could not _____ what information had been lost.

Fill in the blank with the best word from the choices below. One word will not be used.

> exertion   annex   assertion   certitude   obligatory

5.   The _____ with which Angie gave her answer indicated that she felt confident about her knowledge.

6.   Unless the owner can come up with his delinquent mortgage payments in two weeks, the city will _____ his property.

7.   The play was completely predictable, from its conventional opening to its _____ melodramatic ending.

8.   When Alice said that she would win the spelling bee, was she making a confident _____ or just expressing a wish?

Fill in the blank with the best word from the choices below. One word will not be used.

> disconcert   exertion   ligature   annex

9.   Since barely any _____ was required of me at my new job, the muscles I had developed began to weaken.

10. The sudden appearance of Serge, who had been presumed dead in an avalanche, was _____ to the other ski instructors.

11. Because the _____ joining the bird's wing to its body was damaged, the robin was unable to fly.

Exercise III. Choose the set of words that best completes the sentence.

1.   In an attempt to _____ the exact location of the _____ of the two galaxies, the astronomers plotted several points on a graph.
     A. annex; certitude
     B. ascertain; nexus
     C. disconcert; ligature
     D. ascertain; liaison

2.   As long as the request you make does not require much _____ on their part, the employees at the gardening store will respond with _____ politeness.
     A. exertion; obligatory
     B. liaison; disconcerted
     C. nexus; ascertaining
     D. assertion; disconcerted

3.   Momentarily _____ by the disturbance farther up the mountain, Pete became confused, and the _____ joining him to his fellow-climber came undone.
      A.   disconcerted; certitude
      B.   annexed; liaison
      C.   disconcerted; ligature
      D.   ascertained; nexus

4.   Based on their _____ that Aaron could be trusted, the spy organization employed him as a(n) _____ between its agents.
      A.   certitude; liaison
      B.   annex; dissertation
      C.   ligature; assertion
      D.   liaison; certitude

5.   Having made the _____ that no army could defeat his, the general prepared to _____ the neighboring country.
      A.   liaison; disconcert
      B.   dissertation; annex
      C.   assertion; annex
      D.   ligature; ascertain

Exercise IV. Complete the sentence by inferring information about the italicized word from its context.

1.   If Nadine is *disconcerted* by her father's silence, we can infer that she expected…

2.   If Robert is seeking a *liaison* between himself and Nicole, it may be because…

3.   If we are at the *nexus* of the old era and the new, it is probably a time of…

Exercise V. Fill in each blank with the word from the Unit that best completes the sentence, using the root we supply as a clue. Then, answer the questions that follow the paragraphs.

Perhaps the most ironic aspect of such mob organizations as the Mafia is the way in which a code of honor grew to cover an institution based on naked arrogance and gall. Total loyalty was demanded within crime families because the danger from other families was significant and could ultimately be fatal. Yet, when a coup occurred within a particular family, the victor expected to be acclaimed the new leader and supported just as fiercely as the former leader had been—certainly a contradictory way to view the idea of loyalty, since power was usually taken by force.

The way to success in this environment is easy to _____ (CERT). It is achieved through violence, coercion, and fear. Shared guilt becomes a _____ (LIG) that binds families where love used to do the job. The sons of mob leaders are, as small children, shielded from the true sources of the family's income, but as time goes by, pressure is placed on them to kill and become "made men." No relative of someone in the mob can escape the burden of criminal guilt, so no one feels compelled to bring the police into the picture. The theory supports the concept that if everyone is guilty, then everyone will work to avoid detection.

Mob families look much like other upper-middle-class families—nice cars, nice houses, elaborate vacations—but only mob families face, every day, the risk that it might all disappear, that the family's provider might be headed to the morgue or to prison, and that the rest of the family might be exposed to physical or financial risk. Prosperity stolen from others is the easy dream of the mob family; the guilt and the hazards of such a life are its nightmare.

1. The tone of this passage is best described as
    A. regretful.
    B. critical.
    C. realistic.
    D. revealing.

2. What can we infer would happen if guilt were not part of mob families?
    A. The families would no longer see the allure of the mob.
    B. The families would start losing money from their sources of income.
    C. The families would be more vulnerable to betrayal by their own relatives.
    D. The families would pick and choose their loyalties.

3. Which statement best sums up the author's theory of mob loyalty?
    A. Men control the mob through love of family.
    B. False loyalties occur over petty jealousy.
    C. Men in the mob have no loyalty except to their families.
    D. Fear and violence control the mob's loyalty.

Exercise VI. Drawing on your knowledge of roots and words in context, read the following selection and define the italicized words. If you cannot figure out the meaning of the words on your own, look them up in a dictionary. Note that *se* means "apart" and *con* means "together."

Because it is difficult to *secern* the parts of the painting done by de Rameau and those filled in by his students, we can assume that, at some point, students in the school had mastered the special oil techniques taught by their learned supervisor. However, there are certain problems relating to time lapses between de Rameau's lifespan and the founding of the school. My hypothesis *colligates* these diverse facts into what I believe is a unified solution.

UNIT TWELVE

IT, IANC
Latin IRE, ITUM, "to go; to pass"

SEDITION   (sə dish´ ən)   n.   an act or practice aimed at undermining authority; a rebellion
L. *se*, "apart" + *itum = going apart*
The Army general was jailed after being found guilty of spying and *sedition*.
syn: *treason*   ant: *loyalty*

AMBIANCE   (am´ bē əns)   n.   the environment surrounding; the atmosphere
L. *ambi*, "around" + *ire = that which goes around*
We enjoyed the pleasant *ambiance* that our hosts provided when we lived for a week with them.

CIRCUITOUS   (sər kyōō´ i təs)   adj.   roundabout or lengthy
L. *circum*, "around" + *itum = going around*
The forty-five minute drive to Grandmother's took two hours this morning because Dad chose a *circuitous* route that he called "scenic."
syn: *meandering*   ant: *direct, straightforward*

TRANSITORY   (tran´ sə tôr ē)   adj.   short-lived or temporary
L. *trans*, "across" + *itum = going across; passing*
The sandstorm was a *transitory* phenomenon that could be observed for only a few hours.
syn: *momentary*   ant: *permanent, lasting*

CED
Latin CEDERE, CESSUM, "to go; to yield"

ACCEDE   (ak sēd´)   v.   to agree, often at the urging of another
L. *ad*, "toward" + *cedere = to yield toward*
Even though it was a low offer, the owner reluctantly *acceded* to the sale of the family business.
syn: *acquiesce*   ant: *refuse, disagree*

ANTECEDENT   (an tə sē´ dənt)   n.   a preceding event, cause, or condition
L. *ante*, "before" + *cedere = going before*
Dante's knee injury was an *antecedent* to the leg damage that put him in a wheelchair.

PRECEDENT (pres´ ə dənt) *n.* a tradition; an act or decision that is used as a model for future acts or decisions
L. *pre*, "prior to" + *cedere* = *going prior to*
By serving for only two terms, George Washington set a *precedent* for presidents who came after him.

VEN

Latin VENIRE, VENTUM, "to come; to arrive"

CONTRAVENE (kän trə vēn´) *v.* to violate or go against
L. *contra*, "against" + *venire* = *to come against*
Kyle was informed that he had *contravened* company policy by making personal calls during his working hours.
syn: refute, reject   *ant: agree, accept*

ADVENTITIOUS (ad ven´ ti shəs) *adj.* accidental; acquired
L. *ad*, "toward" + *ventum* = *coming toward*
It was difficult to say whether the change in Jackie's personality was natural or *adventitious*.
syn: unplanned

PARVENU (pär´ və nōō) *n.* someone newly wealthy
L. *per*, "through" + *venire* = *to arrive through (money)*
When the Morgans won the lottery, they quickly became a pair of *parvenus*.
syn: nouveau riche

A PARVENU must CARVE A NEW image for himself.

▥ *While it looks as if* precedent *and* antecedent *are synonyms, this is not quite accurate, even though* ante *and* pre *both mean "before." A* precedent *might be used to determine how a court might rule on a matter, or something brand new to the world might have "no precedent." Antecedent, though, is only grammatical or an incident that happens prior to another incident.*

▥ *Have you ever seen white roots coming out of the stem of a tomato plant just above the ground? Since roots almost always grow underground, these are known as* adventitious *roots. Why do you think this is the case?*

EXERCISES - UNIT TWELVE

Exercise I. Complete the sentence in a way that shows you understand the meaning of the italicized vocabulary word.

1. My siblings and I chose the most *circuitous* route to school because…

2. The *adventitious* skyscraper seemed…

3. Owen was considered a *parvenu* by others in his social circle when…

4. Publishing a pamphlet criticizing the government was once considered *sedition* because…

5. Because he could find no *precedent* for the trial in the history of the US legal system, the judge…

6. In order not to *contravene* the wishes of her mother, Maia…

7. Allison knew that her happiness was *transitory* because…

8. Jonathan *acceded* to Mary's suggestion that he buy a car in order to…

9. Minor squabbles between the two countries were an *antecedent* to…

10. Carly enjoyed the hotel's *ambiance* despite the fact that…

Exercise II. Fill in the blank with the best word from the choices below. One word will not be used.

accede   ambiance   circuitous   contravene   transitory

1. The sergeant was warned that if he _____ the general's orders again, he could be severely disciplined.

2. Because Antonio was so _____ in his explanation of the machine's function, we begged him to get to the point.

3. Employers at the company will _____ to their workers' demands only if a court injunction forces the issue.

4. Signs of spring in the city are _____, appearing here today and across town tomorrow.

Fill in the blank with the best word from the choices below. One word will not be used.

adventitious   sedition   antecedent   circuitous

5.   A shorter work composed by the poet in his youth was a(n) _____ to his lengthy masterpiece.

6.   The astronomers noticed _____ particles that they had not expected to find in the meteorite.

7.   Because he was a participant in many acts of _____, Jared was captured and imprisoned by the presidential forces.

Fill in the blank with the best word from the choices below. One word will not be used.

adventitious   precedent   ambiance   parvenu

8.   Though Darryl's new neighbors call him a(n) _____, he is very comfortable with his new status.

9.   The _____ of the little restaurant brought back memories of my grandmother's kitchen.

10. The announcer marveled that there was no_____ in the history of baseball to the team's amazing winning streak.

Exercise III. Choose the set of words that best completes the sentence.

1.   Any attempt to _____ the demands of the ruthless king was punished as an act of _____.
     A. accede; precedent
     B. contravene; antecedent
     C. contravene; sedition
     D. accede; parvenu

2.   Because his wealth was _____ rather than inherited, Mark was considered a _____.
     A. adventitious; parvenu
     B. transitory; sedition
     C. adventitious; precedent
     D. circuitous; parvenu

3.   The strollers enjoyed the _____ of the park on a summer evening, so they chose a _____ path through it.
     A. ambiance; circuitous
     B. sedition; circuitous
     C. parvenu; transitory
     D. ambiance; adventitious

4.   While most people understand that the unsightly construction area downtown is only _____, they hope
     it will not set a(n) _____ for future public projects.
     A.   ambiance; sedition
     B.   circuitous; parvenu
     C.   adventitious; antecedent
     D.   transitory; precedent

Exercise IV. Complete the sentence by inferring information about the italicized word from its context.

1.   Joe will probably choose a *circuitous* route to work if he…

2.   If Gabriel is accused of acts of *sedition*, he may have done something like…

3.   My little brother usually *accedes* to my wishes, which indicates…

**Exercise V. Fill in each blank with the word from the Unit that best completes the sentence, using the root
     we supply as a clue. Then, answer the questions that follow the paragraphs.**

Spices, precious metals, and exotic trade items—these are a few of the key reasons that the English, Spanish, Portuguese, and French first began exploring the New World. The acquisition of territory and lands and the control over people, however, were the chief priorities of the new national governments. Whereas the countries' kings and queens ruled over their subjects, they themselves were still bound to submit to a higher authority: the Catholic Church. From Rome, the Pope issued what are called "papal bulls," usually concerning lines of ascension or settling land disputes among nobles. During the Age of Exploration, one such bull played a defining role in shaping the future of the Americas.

In the 1400s and 1500s, Spain and Portugal, two devoutly Catholic and expansionist countries, were racing to discover new lands, plant their respective flags, and declare sovereignty. The impetus for a quest may have been cities of gold or a new trade route, but, ultimately, the explorers claimed the new lands for God and country and returned home to receive accolades. When Christopher Columbus arrived home from his voyage to the West Indies, he reported the discovery to both Queen Isabella and his religious leader, the Pope; the Portuguese rulers also took an interest since they believed the New World was within Portuguese territory. Previous papal bulls appeared to have marked the new lands, soon to be called the Americas, within Portugal's right of claim. Aligning himself with his native country, though, Pope Alexander VI issued a new bull, *Inter Caetera*, in 1493, which _____ (VEN) previous agreements, redefining the boundaries and giving the New World to Spain.

Portugal naturally protested, threatening war in the New World. Because the new territories were difficult to defend due to the distance and the lack of trained warriors permanently assigned there, the Spanish were forced to negotiate, and the Treaty of Tordesillas, signed in 1494, once again reconfigured the boundaries of Spain and Portugal and the areas each could claim in the unexplored West.

Both countries _____ (CED) to the new treaty, which gave the area now known as Brazil to Portugal, but Spain still maintained control of the New World. Ironically, despite all of the negotiations, both the treaty and the Papal Bull proved _____ (IT). England, operating outside of both decrees, began colonizing the rest of North America and eventually claimed the new territory for itself. No intercession from the Pope could hinder the English explorers. To this day, however, the culture of Florida retains a Hispanic flavor, and Portuguese is still the official language of Brazil.

1.   How did Pope Alexander help shape the cultures of America?
     A.   His authority prevented countries besides Portugal from entering and claiming the New World.
     B.   He wrote the Treaty of Tordesillas.
     C.   He assigned the new lands to Spain.
     D.   He gave Christopher Columbus the money and ships to explore the West Indies.

2.   Why did Pope Alexander issue a new papal bull?
     A.   Portugal was protesting the previous papal bulls.
     B.   The lands discovered by Columbus were not accounted for in previous decrees.
     C.   The Pope was a friend and supporter of Columbus.
     D.   He was a Spaniard himself, and he wanted to favor his own country.

3.   Why did Spain and Portugal let the Vatican decide where they could expand and explore?
     A.   The Pope was considered a neutral third party who helped resolve disputes.
     B.   They wanted to present a united front to England.
     C.   They did not have the manpower to fight the Vatican.
     D.   They were both primarily Catholic countries.

Exercise VI. Drawing on your knowledge of roots and words in context, read the following selection and define the italicized words. If you cannot figure out the meaning of the words on your own, look them up in a dictionary. Note that *re* means "back; again" and *retro* means "back."

Originally, the seven Burmock brothers shared the vast property their father had bequeathed to them. Gradually, however, most of the brothers gave up their holdings and left to make their own lives in the city. Oliver Burmock had been the sole landholder for many years when his brother Duncan suddenly returned. The *revenant* Duncan claimed that he wanted no share of the family holdings, but Oliver insisted on *retroceding* land to him. Duncan finally accepted, and the farm he started on this land is still in operation today.

UNIT THIRTEEN

CEND, CENS
Latin CENDERE, CENSUM, "to burn"

INCENDIARY (in sen´ dē ər ē) *adj.* inflaming; provoking heat or anger
L. *in*, "into" + *cendere* = *burning into*
As a fire safety precaution, the university banned the use of any *incendiary* devices in dormitories.
syn: flammable

INCENSE (in sens´) *v.* to infuriate; to make passionately angry
L. *in*, "into" + *censum* = *burning into*
Peter had failed three of five courses during the semester, which *incensed* his parents.
syn: enrage   *ant: soothe, calm*

A censer is a vessel used for burning incense in religious services.

FLAM
Latin FLAMMA, "flame"

INFLAMMATORY (in flâm´ ə tô rē) *adj.* arousing anger or strong emotion
L. *in*, "into" + *flamma* = *to burn within*
The public shunned the singer following the *inflammatory* remarks she made about religion.
syn: provocative   *ant: innocuous*

FLAMBOYANT (flâm boy´ ənt) *adj.* intended to attract attention; showy
Anthony was well known for the *flamboyant* costumes he wore while performing in the ice show.
syn: ostentatious, audacious   *ant: plain*

LUSTER, LUSTR
Latin LUSTRARE, LUSTRATUM, "to make bright"

LUSTER (lus´ tər) *n.* a brilliance; a brightness
The *luster* of Henry Ford's vision for the company he founded in 1903 has not been dimmed by the passing of the years.
syn: shine

ILLUSTRIOUS (i lus´ trē əs) *adj.* well-known and distinguished
L. *in*, "on" + *lustrare* = *to shine on*
The guest list for the wedding reception read like a Who's Who of *illustrious* celebrities and world leaders.
syn: eminent, notable   *ant: unknown*

Lustrare originally had connections to Roman religion. It meant "to purify by making bright" and described the cleansing of something in preparation for sacrifice. This is why we have the word lustration, *which means "ceremonial purification," but also* illustrate, *which means "to shed light on; to make clear."*

ILLUSTRATIVE (i lus´ tre tiv) *adj.* descriptive; serving as an example
L. *in*, "into" + *lustratum = into brightness*
Karen hoped that the violence and looting currently raging in the streets of the capital were not *illustrative* of the general state of the city.
syn: representative

FULM, FULG
Latin FULMEN, "lightning, storm"
Latin FULGERE, "flash"

FULMINATE (fəl´ mə nāt) *v.* to attack with words; to denounce
Fred publicly *fulminated* against the lack of pollution controls on local construction companies, which finally caught the attention of the local media.
syn: rail   *ant: praise*

REFULGENT (rə fəl´ jənt) *adj.* brilliantly illuminated; shining
L. *re*, "back" + *fulgere = flashing back*
The *refulgent* temple on the hill proved to be a beacon of hope for the weary travelers.
syn: radiant

FLAGR
Latin FLAGRARE, FLAGRANTUM, "to burn"

FLAGRANT (flā´ grənt) *adj.* noticeably bad or offensive
The team protested that the referee was ignoring the *flagrant* fouls committed by the other team.
syn: grievous

CONFLAGRATION (kän flə grā´ shən) *n.* a large fire
L. *con*, "together" + *flagrantum = burning together*
It took firefighters from three towns nearly nine hours to control the *conflagration* at the storage company.
syn: blaze

The CONFLAGRATION ruined DON'S VACATION.

▥ An illustration *does not have to be a drawing. Just as illustrative is an example, an illustration can be the same thing. It's just a matter of which part of speech you need to use since illustration is a noun and illustrative is an adjective.*

▥ *I have rarely seen anything so flagrantly unscientific as those who believe that they were kidnapped by aliens, taken to a distant planet, and brought back here. They offer no proof except their words.*
—*Anonymous*

EXERCISES - UNIT THIRTEEN

Exercise I. Complete the sentence in a way that shows you understand the meaning of the italicized vocabulary word.

1.   Zachary felt that his success at the spelling bee was *illustrative* of his intelligence because…

2.   Because of the massive *conflagration* in the middle of town…

3.   So many *illustrious* guests were at Marissa's party that…

4.   The mayor was advised that her constant *fulminating* would result in…

5.   Lou claimed that he had not meant to be *inflammatory* when he…

6.   When the speaker began chanting *incendiary* slogans, the crowd…

7.   When Grace saw that Harry's eyes had lost their *luster*, she wondered if…

8.   The child's Halloween costume was so *refulgent* that it made everyone…

9.   Society gossips claimed the bride had been too *flamboyant* because she…

10. The judge said that Jasmine's actions had constituted a *flagrant* violation of safety regulations and…

11. Tasha was so *incensed* by the behavior she saw at the candidates' debate that she…

Exercise II. Fill in the blank with the best word from the choices below. One word will not be used.

incense	illustrative	fulminate	flamboyant	conflagration

1.   By the time the fire truck reached the site, the campfire had become a(n) _____.

2.   Although Jacob claimed to be _____ by the B⁺ he received on his math test, he was actually quite pleased.

3.   The showy cook was given to _____ tricks like juggling lemons and frying three eggs at the same time.

4.   The failure of two businesses was _____ of Hope's belief that the town was headed for economic ruin.

Fill in the blank with the best word from the choices below. One word will not be used.

incendiary   refulgent   luster   conflagration   illustrious

5.   No matter what _____ tactics the rebel leader employed, he could not anger the citizens enough to start a riot in the city.

6.   Witnesses to the supposed miracle described a(n) _____ figure whose brightness was almost blinding.

7.   The _____ of the gold coin was dimmed by years of wear.

8.   Though he had once been considered a(n) _____ figure, Lyle's importance in the community was greatly diminished by the scandal.

Fill in the blank with the best word from the choices below. One word will not be used.

flagrant   fulminate   inflammatory   illustrious

9.   As a therapist, Jeanne tries to steer her patients away from _____ language and hurtful actions.

10.   Chances are good that, even if the law is passed, those who are violently opposed will continue to _____ against it.

11.   Despite his one-time _____ violation of company policy, Todd was awarded Employee of the Year.

Exercise III. Choose the set of words that best completes the sentence.

1.   In my opinion, Oliver's remarks were _____ of the kind of _____ language that has led to many problems in this town.
      A.   illustrative; incendiary
      B.   illustrious; inflammatory
      C.   inflammatory; refulgent
      D.   flamboyant; incendiary

2.   Although the _____ musician drew crowds by virtue of his superb skill, some critics disapproved of his overbearing, _____ personality.
      A.   inflammatory; refulgent
      B.   refulgent; flagrant
      C.   illustrious; flamboyant
      D.   flagrant; illustrious

3.   My _____ words so _____ Carl that he stopped speaking to me for six months.
      A.   illustrious; refulgent
      B.   flagrant; incensed
      C.   inflammatory; incensed
      D.   illustrative; flamboyant

4.   The _____ of the diamond necklace actually seemed to increase as it was placed around the neck of the beautiful girl; it seemed as _____ as the night sky.
     A. luster; refulgent
     B. conflagration; inflammatory
     C. luster; flagrant
     D. conflagration; incendiary

5.   The president of the local school board _____ against the band's lyrics on the grounds that they were obscene, prompting a huge _____ in which copies of the work were burned.
     A. incensed; luster
     B. fulminated; conflagration
     C. incensed; conflagration
     D. fulminated; luster

Exercise IV. Complete the sentence by inferring information about the italicized word from its context.

1.   As a punishment for her *flagrant* violation of the law, Cindy may be sentenced to…

2.   If Nathan writes and distributes an *incendiary* pamphlet, he is probably trying to…

3.   Upon catching sight of a massive *conflagration* a few miles from her home, Natasha may worry that…

Exercise V. Fill in each blank with the word from the Unit that best completes the sentence, using the root we supply as a clue. Then, answer the questions that follow the paragraphs.

Born in 1810, Phineas Taylor (P. T.) Barnum was one of the most _____ (FLAM) showmen of all time. He was not a performer, but an expert at promotion and advertising. He delighted in the "art of the humbug," which he used as a means of tricking his customers. Rather than angering his audience, however, Barnum's consummate showmanship made them want to come back for more.

Barnum's career presenting the strange and unusual started in the 1830s, when he began promoting appearances by Joice Heth, an African American woman whom Barnum billed as being George Washington's 160-year-old childhood nurse. Although Heth's personal appearances were quite popular, when she died a few years later, she was found to be, in fact, only 70 years old.

While touring the country and presenting Joice Heth, Barnum found his calling as a master huckster and discovered that there was a great deal of money to be made in the entertainment business. Three years after Heth's death, Barnum created the American Museum in New York City. The museum was the first of its kind and quickly became one of the city's most popular attractions. It contained a collection of fascinating scientific specimens, but it also presented a variety of freakish, odd, and outlandish displays that appealed to middle-class Americans of the mid-1800s. Barnum's museum was filled with catchy, flashy, and confusing gimmicks to either draw in customers or make them part with more of their money. These were Barnum's humbugs, and they have become part of entertainment history.

One famous element of the American Museum is now a show business legend. Once in the museum, customers would see many colorful and eye-catching signs that stated, "This way to the egress." Giving in to the hype, customers became curious. They followed the signs through the museum to the "egress," many hoping to see another curio, beast, or freak of nature. Once at the "egress," customers opened the door, walked through, and found themselves outside the museum building. If they wished to return to the museum, they had to pay a second entrance fee. Rather than becoming _____ (CENS) at being tricked out of their money, patrons of the American Museum joined Barnum in the joke. In fact, customers would often return with their friends so that they, too, could be tricked. Patrons knew that Barnum's approach to entertainment was to intrigue and entertain. The _____ (LUSTER) of this type of entertainment has never faded.

In 1865, P. T. Barnum's American Museum fell victim to a terrible _____ (FLAGR), and it burned to the ground. Barnum spent a few years in financial difficulty, but then he got the idea to mount another national tour, which would present an array of curiosities and performers. He teamed with a partner named Bailey to present a traveling show. The Ringling Brothers, who later bought the show, continued to use Barnum's name for promotional purposes. To this day, the most famous circus in the world retains the name of Ringling Bros. and Barnum & Bailey. It also keeps the title bestowed upon it by P. T. Barnum himself. It remains "the greatest show on earth."

1.   Which of the following sentences best presents the main idea of the passage?
     A.   P. T. Barnum was the founder of the Ringling Bros. and Barnum & Bailey circus.
     B.   P. T. Barnum often tricked people out of their money.
     C.   P. T. Barnum was a master promoter and showman.
     D.   P. T. Barnum's American Museum was a unique part of pop culture in the mid-1800s.

2.   A humbug is a
     A.   type of traveling show.
     B.   type of museum display.
     C.   form of popular entertainment in the 19th century.
     D.   hoax or fraud.

3.   Upon the death of Joice Heth, it was found that she could not have been George Washington's nurse, as Barnum declared, because she was
     A.   the same age as Washington.
     B.   too young.
     C.   never a nurse.
     D.   touring the country with Barnum during George Washington's childhood.

4.   According to the article, P. T. Barnum's greatest and most enduring contribution to American entertainment was the
     A.   American Museum.
     B.   creation of flashy showmanship.
     C.   modern museum.
     D.   creation of Ringling Bros. and Barnum & Bailey circus.

Exercise VI. Drawing on your knowledge of roots and words in context, read the following selection and define the italicized words. If you cannot figure out the meaning of the words on your own, look them up in a dictionary. Note that *de*, in this case, means "very."

The *fulgurating* skies of late August provided some free entertainment this afternoon. Mother and Wally came out onto the porch from the living room, where they had been watching soap operas, and seated themselves to view the pulsing electricity arc across the sky. Soon, several of Wally's brothers returned from the fields, expressing concern that the wheat, already dry from months without rain, would *deflagrate* rapidly if the lightning struck the field.

UNIT FOURTEEN

SEMA, SEMIO
Greek SEMA, "sign"

SEMANTIC (sə mân´ tək) *adj.* having to do with the meaning of words or
    language
If we judge the poem strictly on a *semantic* basis, rather than noting its emotional
and sensory impact, it will seem to make no sense.

SEMIOTIC (sə mē o´ tək) *adj.* of or relating to signs or symbols
For slaves fleeing to Canada, the North Star had a *semiotic* function, as well as a
practical one: it symbolized hope and freedom.

DIGM, DICT
Greek DIGMA, "a showing; a comparison"

PARADIGM (pa´ rə dīm) *n.* a pattern or model
G. *para*, "alongside" + *digma* = *to show alongside; to compare*
The elections this year seem to be following the conventional *paradigm*.

PHRAS
Greek PHRASEIN, "to show; to tell"

PHRASEOLOGY (frā zē o´ lə gē) *n.* the way in which something is expressed;
    a style
G. *phrasein* + *ology*, "study of, practice of" = *the practice of telling*
Kim's *phraseology* was a good indication that she had spent years in boarding
school.

METAPHRASE (me´ tə frāz) *n.* an exact translation or restatement
G. *meta*, "after" + *phrasein* = *to tell after; to restate*
Mr. Keating was disappointed to find that his best student's paper was a complete
metaphrase of a passage from an old library book.

PARAPHRASE (pa´ rə frāz) *n.* a summary that is not word-for-word
G. *para*, "beside" + *phrasein* = *to tell beside; to summarize*
A short *paraphrase* of the play was provided in the program for audience
members who were unfamiliar with the work.
syn: précis

Semaphore (sema + phorein, "to bear") is a system of signs made using flags and specific hand positions. Each letter of the alphabet is represented by a different position, and many signs can also symbolize entire words.

Do not confuse sema, semio with the more common semi, which means "half," as in semicolon.

Your research paper writing will always be acceptable if you paraphrase material correctly, and you won't be accused of plagiarism, which comes from the Latin plagiarus, "kidnapper."

MONSTR
Latin MONSTRARE, MONSTRATUM, "to show; to warn"

DEMONSTRATIVE   (di mon´ strə tiv)   *adj.*   openly expressive of emotions
L. *de*, "very, completely" + *monstratum = to show completely*
Though Esther was not usually *demonstrative*, she wept openly at her uncle's funeral.

REMONSTRATE   (rə´ mon strāt)   *v.*   to protest or object
L. *re*, "back" + *monstratum = to show back*
Irma *remonstrated* against the tax hike, saying she could barely survive at the current rate.

OMIN
Latin OMEN, "sign; warning"

OMINOUS   (om´ ə nəs)   *adj.*   menacing; threatening
When the *ominous* gray clouds began to roll across the plains, the farmhands ran to find shelter.

ABOMINABLE   (ə bom´ ə nə bəl)   *adj.*   loathsome; disagreeable
L. *ab*, "away from" + *omen = to move away from a bad omen*
The *abominable* condition of the stables showed us that Mike had been neglecting his chores.

ABOMINATION   (ə bom ə nā´ shən)   *n.*   something disgustingly offensive
The newspapers described Wendy's obnoxious behavior the other night as "an *abomination* to the office of US ambassador."

The protestors felt it would be an ABOMINATION to A-BOMB A NATION.

Ⅲ *Many actors are too demonstrative—they overact. This faulty technique is known as "chewing the scenery," meaning that emotions are revealed through overly dramatic movements, yelling, crying, etc., essentially by telling an audience what the actor feels, rather than allowing the audience to figure it out.*

Ⅲ *If you want to be fully convinced of the abominations of slavery, go on a southern plantation, and call yourself a slave trader.*
—Harriet Jacobs, author of Incidents in the Life of a Slave Girl

EXERCISES - UNIT FOURTEEN

Exercise I. Complete the sentence in a way that shows you understand the meaning of the italicized vocabulary word.

1.   Halle decided to *paraphrase* the article in her speech rather than...

2.   Investigators considered the suspect's increase in wealth an *ominous* sign of...

3.   Many believed that the famous stadium had a *semiotic* value because...

4.   In order to study the social *paradigms* in the small town, the researchers...

5.   Olivia chose not to *remonstrate* with the server, even though...

6.   The king's reign was thought to be an *abomination* that...

7.   Because Vanessa was such a *demonstrative* actress, critics said that she...

8.   Fighter pilots utilize a specialized *phraseology* to...

9.   Although Jeff and Corey argued about the *semantic* qualities of their favorite songs,...

10.   Even though he had done some truly *abominable* things, the General...

11.   Greg did not want a *metaphrase* of Sam's conversation with Melissa because...

Exercise II. Fill in the blank with the best word from the choices below. One word will not be used.

    remonstrate   metaphrase   semiotic   paradigm   ominous

1.   The ship's crew considered the rough water _____; it signaled the approach of violent winds.

2.   If the county builds a highway through the residential neighborhood, local citizens will surely _____.

3.   Designers of wartime propaganda had to be acutely aware of the _____ impact of the objects depicted in their posters.

4.   The educational _____ will be radically changed by the ideas that Professor Davis has introduced.

Fill in the blank with the best word from the choices below. One word will not be used.

semantic   abominable   demonstrative   paraphrase   phraseology

5.   It is easy to see how Roger could misinterpret the passage on a(n) _____ level; its meaning has bewildered scholars for centuries.

6.   The _____ of the business world was developed to maximize efficiency in speaking.

7.   The cut that Christina's new hairdresser gave her was so _____ that Christina left the salon in tears.

8.   It was clear that Perry had based his paper on the brief _____ on the book's back cover, rather than the book itself.

Fill in the blank with the best word from the choices below. One word will not be used.

demonstrative   paradigm   abomination   metaphrase

9.   Because the sisters were very shy, their aunt's _____ behavior made them uncomfortable.

10. I agree that George's theft of your pencil was wrong, but I would not say it was a(n) "_____ before God," as you did.

11. Señora Otavio asked for an interpretation of the passage, not a(n) _____.

Exercise III. Choose the set of words that best completes the sentence.

1.   Isaiah worked hard for several years on a(n) _____ of an ancient text, and he was devastated when some scholars called his version _____.
     A. metaphrase; demonstrative
     B. abomination; semiotic
     C. paradigm; semantic
     D. metaphrase; abominable

2.   While your _____ conveys the poem's _____ properties, it fails to deal with its emotional impact.
     A. paradigm; demonstrative
     B. paraphrase; semantic
     C. abomination; semiotic
     D. phraseology; ominous

3.   If art historians can understand the _____ significance of the strange painting, they can better grasp the social and cultural _____ of the time in which it was created.
     A. ominous; metaphrase
     B. semiotic; paradigm
     C. demonstrative; phraseology
     D. semantic; paraphrase

4. Because the children had been worried about the emotional pressure their usually shy father was under, they considered his newly _____ behavior a(n) _____ sign.
    A. demonstrative; ominous
    B. ominous; semantic
    C. abominable; demonstrative
    D. semantic; demonstrative

5. Lovers of the classical style of singing may consider the muffled, slurred _____ employed by today's musicians a(n) _____.
    A. abomination; paradigm
    B. paradigm; phraseology
    C. phraseology; abomination
    D. paraphrase; phraseology

Exercise IV. Complete the sentence by inferring information about the italicized word from its context.

1. If Neela *remonstrates* with her sister, we can assume her sister has…

2. If there is a major change in the country's economic *paradigm*, the result may be…

3. Critics have generally concluded that the film is an *abomination*; potential viewers should probably…

Exercise V. Fill in each blank with the word from the Unit that best completes the sentence, using the root we supply as a clue. Then, answer the questions that follow the paragraphs.

Queen Christina of Sweden was born on December 8, 1626, in Stockholm. Centuries later, she would be described as "one of history's greatest rebels" by the director of Stockholm's National Museum of Fine Arts. Her most infamous "rebellion," however, was against the unwritten but strict laws of gender in the 17th century.

The only child of King Gustav II and Maria Eleonora, Christina was the heir to Sweden's throne, and her father insisted on raising her as though she were a prince. To this end, in addition to studying politics, philosophy, and languages twelve hours a day, Christina enthusiastically trained in sports and hunting. Her mother, ironically disgusted both that Christina had not been born a male and that Christina was not more feminine, considered her daughter an _____ (OMIN).

Christina's royal education had begun none too soon. When she was five, her father died in the Thirty Years' War, and she became the queen-elect. Although chancellor Axel Oxenstierna led the country until Christina came of legal age, Christina began to attend council meetings and unofficially govern at age thirteen. In her spare time, she learned to read and speak in five languages, began to seriously question religion, and enjoyed riding and bear-hunting. She continued to be _____ (MONSTR) about her distaste for traditionally feminine activities, wearing men's clothing and stating "an ineradicable prejudice against everything that women like to talk about or do."

At eighteen, Christina was formally crowned, and friction began to grow between her and Oxenstierna. Christina denounced the Thirty Years' War, although the chancellor and many other powerful people approved of it. She was instrumental in concluding the Peace of Westphalia, which ended the war. A country at peace left Christina free for other pursuits, among them a great push to make Stockholm an "Athens of the North." She sponsored artists and musicians, financed theatre and opera performances, and invited specialists from all branches of intellectual study to Stockholm. She also helped to create the first Swedish newspaper. Her intellectual daring and liveliness seemed boundless.

In her mid-twenties, however, Christina suffered a breakdown. She was under intense pressure to marry her cousin Charles Gustavus in order to produce an heir to the throne. Wedded to her independence, Christina was unwilling to consign herself to marriage and went so far as to say that she would not marry even if it meant that she would become ruler of the world.

When she regained her health, Christina renounced her throne, giving the crown to Charles rather than marrying him, and the former Queen quickly departed Sweden for Rome. Unconventional to the last, when she left, she did so on horseback, dressed as a knight.

1. The main idea of this passage is that Queen Christina
    A. disappointed her public.
    B. challenged the gender norms of the 17th century.
    C. did not accomplish much during her reign.
    D. did not like the idea of marriage.

2. Which of the following unconventional things did Christina NOT do?
    A. dressed in men's clothing
    B. agitate for peace during a popular war
    C. banish her mother from Stockholm
    D. question religion

3. The phrase "Athens of the North" probably refers to
    A. cultural and intellectual pursuits in Stockholm.
    B. bringing the Olympic games to Stockholm.
    C. the building of a stronger army in Sweden.
    D. the return to a polytheistic religion in Sweden.

4. Christina and Oxenstierna clashed because he
    A. thought Christina should be more regal.
    B. was jealous of Christina's birthright.
    C. did not approve of liberal intellectuals.
    D. did not want the Thirty Years' War to end.

Exercise VI. Drawing on your knowledge of roots and words in context, read the following selection and define the italicized words. If you cannot figure out the meaning of the words on your own, look them up in a dictionary. Note that *apo* means "from" and *peri* means "around."

Tight-lipped President Coolidge tended to stick to *apodictic* statements; if he had to discuss something that he did not absolutely know to be true, he was very uncomfortable. In addition, he shunned all kinds of *periphrasis* and hesitancy in speaking. Every question received a direct answer or no answer at all. It is no wonder he got a reputation for being both reserved and strictly honest.

UNIT FIFTEEN

TRIT
Latin TERERE, TRITUS, "to rub away; to wear; to crush"

DETRIMENTAL   (det rə men´ təl)   *adj.*   causing damage or harm; injurious
L. *de*, "away" + *tritus* = *rubbing away from*
Physicians are divided as to whether the drug is *detrimental* to a patient's nervous system or not.

                                ant: helpful, beneficial

CONTRITE   (kən trīt´)   *adj.*   feeling regret and sorrow; penitent
The defendant was *contrite* at the sentencing hearing, offering apologies to the family of his victim.

TRITE   (trīt)   *adj.*   boring because of overuse or repetition
The lyrics of the song are *trite*, even sappy, but it remains a popular favorite.
syn: clichéd　　　　　　　　　　　　*ant: original*

DETRITUS   (də trī´ təs)   *n.*   debris; junk
L. *de*, "off" + *tritus* = *that which has been rubbed off*
When the sailors noticed unusual *detritus* floating in front of their ship, they wondered if they had reached land.
syn: flotsam

ATTRITION   (ə trish´ ən)   *n.*   a gradual lowering in number
L. *ad*, "toward, against" + *tritus* = *worn against*
The high teacher *attrition* in the school led the principal to seek new employees at the local college.

The ADDITION of NUTRITION halted
the population's ATTRITION.

▥ *Conterere, the word from which* contrite *ultimately comes, originally meant "to grind." Someone who is* contrite *has been worn down by regret or grief to the point that he or she repents or apologizes.*

▥ *Phrases that today are considered* trite *were once new and fresh. "A wild goose chase," "full circle," and "dead as a doornail," all of which are overused clichés, sounded brand new to Elizabethan audiences when Shakespeare first wrote them into his plays.*

LENI
Latin LENIS, "smooth"

LENIENT (lē´ nyənt) *adj.* not strict; generous
Millie liked to stay over at Fran's house because Fran's parents were *lenient* about bedtimes.

LENITIVE (lə´ nə təv) *adj.* easing pain or discord
Sarah's soothing personality had a *lenitive* effect at tense, argument-filled business meetings.

MOLL
Latin MOLLIS, "soft"

MOLLIFY (mo´ lə fī) *v.* to soothe the feelings of; to appease
Although Ingrid had been insulted by some of the things Ben had said about her, she was *mollified* by his letter of apology.

RUD
Latin RUDIS, "rough"

RUDIMENT (rōō´ də mənt) *n.* a basic idea or principle
Once you have learned the *rudiments* of chess, you will be ready to enter a beginners' tournament.

RUDIMENTARY (rōō də mən´ tə rē) *adj.* undeveloped; very basic or simple
Even a *rudimentary* book on the French language contains some information on art and culture, so I was surprised that my advanced book had nothing to say on the subject.
syn: primitive   *ant: advanced*

⬛ *An emollient (e, "out," + mollis = to soften out) is a cream or lotion applied to the skin to make it softer.*

⬛ *Philosophy is such a complex subject that it is sometimes better to have only a rudimentary knowledge of it so as not to embarrass yourself in conversation by expressing too much misinformation thinking it is a correct analysis of, say, Leibniz or Descartes.*
—Anonymous

EXERCISES - UNIT FIFTEEN

Exercise I. Complete the sentence in a way that shows you understand the meaning of the italicized vocabulary word.

1.   The *attrition* of state troopers was due in large part to…

2.   I could tell that Fran was feeling *contrite* about the argument because she…

3.   The clerk was unable to *mollify* the angry customer because…

4.   The protesters argued that a ban on handguns would be *detrimental* to society because…

5.   Because Ally was *lenient* with her sister's children, they often…

6.   When the actor used a *trite* phrase to describe his happiness about the new film, many members of the media…

7.   Tim said that Andrew's math skills were *rudimentary* because…

8.   The *detritus* in the yard was a result of…

9.   The drug's *lenitive* effect on Albert's condition made him wonder if…

10.   Because she knew the *rudiments* of the complicated dance, Nancy was able to…

Exercise II. Fill in the blank with the best word from the choices below. One word will not be used.

mollify   detritus   attrition   rudiment   detrimental

1.   Paul believed that a diet that included artificial sweeteners and preservatives would be _____ to his health and perhaps even shorten his life.

2.   Seeking to _____ his bawling little sister, Denny handed her several cookies.

3.   Edie is just learning the _____ of music, but her brother is an advanced piano student.

4.   Because jobs and relationships in other parts of the country beckoned us, my grandfather faced the slow _____ of his large family.

Fill in the blank with the best word from the choices below. One word will not be used.

       rudimentary   lenient   detritus   lenitive

5.   A once-prized wooden toy had now become one more bit of _____ bobbing at the lake's edge.

6.   Leah urged the judge to be more _____ with her client, who had committed no previous crimes.

7.   Investigators were dismayed to learn that their understanding of the complex criminal network was _____ at best.

Fill in the blank with the best word from the choices below. One word will not be used.

       contrite   rudiment   lenitive   trite

8.   Hannah wanted to get a greeting card that was funny and original instead of _____ and boring.

9.   Bob found that the solution given to him by the veterinarian had a _____ effect on the kitten's irritated eye.

10.   Because Zachary did not seem at all _____ about bullying his sister, his mother grounded him for three days.

Exercise III. Choose the set of words that best completes the sentence.

1.   Landon warned that being too _____ with the dogs could actually be _____ to their health.
    A. contrite; lenitive
    B. lenient; detrimental
    C. rudimentary; trite
    D. lenient; rudimentary

2.   Henry was sincerely _____ about losing my favorite hat, and the replacement he bought had a _____ effect on my anger.
    A. lenient; rudimentary
    B. contrite; mollifying
    C. detrimental; lenient
    D. trite; mollifying

3.   Someone with even a _____ knowledge of poetry would understand how _____ and unoriginal the last line of the sonnet is.
    A. detrimental; contrite
    B. trite; lenitive
    C. lenitive; detrimental
    D. rudimentary; trite

4. Despite the _____ effect of the pay raise, the _____ rate among teachers continues to rise.
   A. lenitive; attrition
   B. lenient; detritus
   C. contrite; rudiment
   D. trite; attrition

5. Having mastered the _____ of sailing, Terence could maneuver his little craft skillfully enough to avoid _____ in the river.
   A. detritus; attrition
   B. attrition; rudiments
   C. detritus; rudiments
   D. rudiments; detritus

Exercise IV. Complete the sentence by inferring information about the italicized word from its context.

1. If a class promises to teach the *rudiments* of bowling, a good bowler should probably…

2. Because Greg is acting *contrite* about the relay race, we can assume he…

3. If Ashley says that her speech at the convention had a *lenitive* effect, it is probably true that before her speech…

Exercise V. Fill in each blank with the word from the Unit that best completes the sentence, using the root we supply as a clue. Then, answer the questions that follow the paragraphs.

World War II occurred after a series of regional conflicts culminated in Hitler's invasion of Poland in 1939. It ended when Japan ceased fighting in August of 1945. The war lasted only six years, which is not long as history goes, but it produced the biggest armies, the longest battlefronts, the most demanding logistical challenges, and the most awesome weapons of any war up to its time. It inflicted more suffering, destroyed more, and cost more than any other war. Some of the victims and participants of World War I were still alive at the outset of World War II and were able to remember the losses they endured and the terrible tragedies their countries suffered. It didn't seem possible leaders could once again bring their people to the brink of extinction with another war of _____ (TRIT). Millions of people would serve their countries, and millions more would be slaughtered indiscriminately.

The ancient cities of Europe and Asia were targets of unimaginable devastation. Firebombing raids caused what resembled Dante's *Inferno* on Earth. Whole industrial centers and population centers were razed. The atomic bombs reduced Hiroshima and Nagasaki to piles of radioactive rubble. The social, cultural, and technological changes brought about by the war were enormous. They included the Communist growth and dominance in Eastern Europe, Japan and Germany being ruled by foreign powers, and an entire generation of young men decimated by the rigors of a war.

The United States fought to win and win we did. We fought to destroy a monstrous evil threatening our very civilization. If you are interested, the horrors of World War II can still be witnessed in the museums and the national cemeteries of the countries involved. You still have time to talk to family members who were participants and hear firsthand how they managed to endure those terrible years and live to tell of the War's _____ (TRIT) effects. It is important that we understand how world wars happen so we can do our best to avoid repeating our mistakes. World War II continues to live in the hearts and minds of its survivors.

1.   According to the passage, how was World War II different from other wars?
      A. People were brought to the "brink of extinction."
      B. It "inflicted more suffering" and cost more.
      C. The "cities of Europe and Asia" were destroyed.
      D. The US fought to destroy "a monstrous evil."

2.   The author encourages the reader to learn more about World War II because
      A. it was so horrendous.
      B. it was short compared to other wars.
      C. knowledge can prevent us from repeating past mistakes.
      D. we can gather firsthand accounts of the war.

3.   A phrase that best describes the tone of this passage is
      A. respectful but sad.
      B. patriotic and proud.
      C. proud and concerned.
      D. respectful and patriotic.

4.   What source of information about World War II does the author mention?
      A. history books
      B. personal accounts
      C. newspaper articles
      D. documentary films

Exercise VI. Drawing on your knowledge of roots and words in context, read the following selection and define the italicized words. If you cannot figure out the meaning of the words on your own, look them up in a dictionary.

   In addition to risk of serious injury, coal miners forced into the dangerous crevices beneath the earth were guaranteed chronic illness by the unhealthy atmosphere. Though they *moiled* away in the mines for days, months, years, and decades at a time, the solid rock never got any softer or easier to move. Instead, human backs, arms, fingers, and legs were damaged and broken. *Triturated* coal made its way into the lungs, causing cancer and emphysema. This dust also stuck to the miners' helmets, boots, and skin.

UNIT SIXTEEN

PLIC
Latin PLICARE, PLICATUM, "to fold"
Latin PLEX, PLICIS, "fold"

IMPLICIT   (im pli′ sit)   *adj.*   implied or understood but not directly expressed
L. *in*, "in" + *plicare* = *folded in*
Abigail and John had an *implicit* agreement to never raise the subject of politics at her mother's house.

INEXPLICABLE   (in eks plik′ ə bəl)   *adj.*   difficult or impossible to explain
L. *in*, "not" + *ex*, "out" + *plicare* = *not able to be folded out*
I found Yolanda's refusal to carry an umbrella *inexplicable.*
syn: undefinable   *ant: clear*

John's behavior was both DESPICABLE and INEXPLICABLE.

VERG
Latin VERGERE, "to bend; to turn toward"

DIVERGE   (dī vərj′)   *v.*   to branch out; to go different ways
L. *dis*, "apart" + *vergere* = *to bend apart*
The two sisters agreed on many things, but their opinions *diverged* on the subject of raising children.
syn: split, divide   *ant: converge*

CONVERGE   (kən vərj′)   *v.*   to come together; to gather; to meet
L. *con*, "together" + *vergere* = *to bend together*
Every year, the motorcycle club *converges* on the town for a peaceful gathering.
syn: join   *ant: deviate*

CLIV
Latin CLIVUS, "slope"

ACCLIVITY   (ə kliv′ ə tē)   *n.*   a climbing slope; a hill
L. *ad*, "toward" + *clivus* = *slope toward*
The observatory stands at the foot of a gentle *acclivity* that leads to a scenic overlook.
         ant: decline

Most people are familiar with pliers, the household tool used to grasp and pull. The verb ply *comes from* plicare *and means not only "to grasp, to pull," but also "to give favors to in order to achieve something." For instance, you might* ply *a stubborn child with candy.*

If someone enjoys climbing mountains and skiing down them, you might say he or she has a proclivity *for both* acclivity *and* declivity.

DECLIVITY   (dē kliv´ ə tē)   *n.*   a downward slope; a dip
L. *de*, "down" + *clivus* = *downward slope*
The general chose a broad *declivity* in the landscape as the place where the army could take shelter for the night.

PROCLIVITY   (prō kliv´ ə tē)   *n.*   a natural tendency toward
L. *pro*, "forward, toward" + *clivus* = *leaning toward*
Kyle's *proclivity* for tennis was in keeping with his natural athletic ability.
syn: predisposition, bent

TORT
Latin TORQUERE, TORTUM, "to twist"

CONTORT   (kon tôrt´)   *v.*   to twist, wrench, or bend severely out of shape
L. *con*, "together" + *tortum* = *to twist together*
Brenda was able to *contort* her body and touch her head with her toes.

DISTORT   (dis tôrt´)   *v.*   to misshape; to misrepresent
L. *dis*, "apart" + *tortum* = *to twist apart*
Critics felt that the film unjustly *distorted* the role of private school education in Massachusetts.
syn: pervert

SIN
Latin SINUS, "curve"

SINUOUS   (sin´ ū əs)   *adj.*   curving or twisting
As the car moved past the mountains, we saw the *sinuous* road become a flat, straight highway.
syn: writhing

INSINUATE   (in sin´ ū āt)   *v.*   to suggest in an indirect or subtle fashion
L. *in*, "into" + *sinus* = *curving into*
When Joe asked why I had missed his party, was he *insinuating* that I had secretly been meeting Julia?
syn: hint, imply

In addition to these two, other tortum words also have the meaning of "twist": extort, torture, retort, tortuous, distort, torsion, *and* torque. *But the foods* tortellini *and* tortilla, *which seem like they should be related, are actually from the Latin* torta, *meaning "cake."*

You may have been given a sine *curve to graph in your math class. Since* sine *comes directly from* sinus *and literally means "curve," the term "sine* curve" *is actually redundant.*

EXERCISES – UNIT SIXTEEN

Exercise I. Complete the sentence in a way that shows you understand the meaning of the italicized vocabulary word.

1.   The author admitted that he had *distorted* events in his retelling of the story, but said it was because…

2.   Because Randall's taste in music rarely *diverged* from his father's, people thought…

3.   Noting the *sinuous* channel the lava had carved in the hill, researchers guessed that…

4.   Considering Rebecca's *proclivity* for public speaking, it is remarkable that…

5.   Though Anne felt that the right to veto any decision had been *implicit* in her contract, her coworkers…

6.   Millions of shorebirds *converge* upon the lake every year in order to…

7.   A noticeable *acclivity* in the carpet was the result of…

8.   Because he did not notice the *declivity* in the road ahead, Jake…

9.   When Vince *insinuated* that he had been responsible for his basketball team's success, his coach…

10.   When Sue Ellen saw Jamie's face *contort*, she wondered if…

11.   Doctors found the change in Jack's condition *inexplicable* because…

Exercise II. Fill in the blank with the best word from the choices below. One word will not be used.

contort	sinuous	converge	inexplicable	acclivity

1.   Given the recent labor shortage, the sudden round of firings at the chicken plant is
_____ .

2.   City officials are worried that crowds of people arriving for the rock concert will _____
on the nearby town and cause damage to people's property.

3.   Because there were dangerous corals to avoid, the swimmer was forced to take a(n)
_____ path to the island.

4.   The shifting of the landscape during the earthquake caused a small _____ where the
ground had been level and flat.

Fill in the blank with the best word from the choices below. One word will not be used.

insinuate   declivity   implicit   contort   diverge

5.   Though the two art styles had a common origin, they _____ at the turn of the nineteenth century.

6.   In an effort to imitate her uptight, sour-natured band director, Monica _____ her face into a lopsided frown.

7.   Prime Minister O'Connell asked defensively if the reporter were _____ something negative about the current government policy.

8.   Pushed by her sister, Annabelle toppled down the _____ and rolled for several hundred yards.

Fill in the blank with the best word from the choices below. One word will not be used.

implicit   distort   proclivity   sinuous

9.   I believe I have a(n) _____ for politics because I care about current issues, and I love being around people.

10.   _____ in the speech about forgiving others was the idea that we must forgive ourselves.

11.   Because Nicole's view was _____ by the sheet of driving rain, the buildings on the horizon seemed warped and wobbly.

Exercise III. Choose the set of words that best completes the sentence.

1.   Though the article _____ that the actress has a gambling addiction, we must keep in mind that the magazine in which it appears is known for _____ the facts.
    A. diverges; contorting
    B. contorts; insinuating
    C. insinuates; distorting
    D. diverges; converges

2.   Because neither Marjorie nor Nicolas was the slightest bit musical, they found their son's _____ for the violin _____.
    A. acclivity; implicit
    B. proclivity; inexplicable
    C. proclivity; sinuous
    D. declivity; inexplicable

3.   Jack's faith in Tara is _____ in everything he says, and his opinion hardly ever _____ from hers.
      A.   sinuous; converges
      B.   implicit; diverges
      C.   inexplicable; insinuates
      D.   implicit; contorts

4.   At one moment the dancer would _____ himself into a small, hunched figure; at the next, his body would open into _____ twists and spirals.
      A.   insinuate; implicit
      B.   converge; sinuous
      C.   contort; sinuous
      D.   distort; inexplicable

5.   The point at which the roads _____ marks the bottom of the _____ down which the river used to tumble.
      A.   contort; proclivity
      B.   converge; acclivity
      C.   insinuate; declivity
      D.   converge; declivity

Exercise IV. Complete the sentence by inferring information about the italicized word from its context.

1.   If Marie wants to *insinuate* that Karen is not a hard worker, she may say something like…

2.   If the student's opinion *diverges* from that of his professor, it may be because…

3.   When the structural engineer says that the building's collapse was *inexplicable*, we can infer that he expected…

Exercise V. Fill in each blank with the word from the Unit that best completes the sentence, using the root we supply as a clue. Then, answer the questions that follow the paragraphs.

The Russian Revolution, which had and continues to have a profound effect on world history in the twentieth century, actually took place in three distinct stages. The first of these occurred in 1905, after the defeat of Russia in the Russo-Japanese War. The defeat became a catalyst for a broad range of social grievances aimed at the existing autocratic czarist social order. A massacre of workers marching on Czar Nicholas II's Winter Palace with a petition demanding social reforms led to widespread insurrections throughout the country among workers, peasants, and the military. This unrest was stemmed for a time by a halfhearted and desperate attempt on the part of the czarist government to rectify some of the conditions that had produced the uprisings. The reforms, however, fell short, as the existing governmental structure proved too entrenched and unwilling to relinquish power. The royal family's _____ (PLIC) blindness to the gathering forces of history led to the next phase of

the Communist takeover, which culminated in the bloody conflict of World War I.

When war broke out in 1914, the country at first rallied around the czar's government. As the war dragged on and military reverses accumulated, however, a growing chorus demanded that the government become more responsive to the public. The war also produced an increasing economic strain on the nation, as resources were drained away to support the war effort. Strikes by discontented workers and the complaints of starving millions in food lines led to increasing calls for an end to czarist rule. When soldiers sent to put down a Moscow uprising mutinied to join the protesters, the czar was forced to abdicate, and a Provisional Government was formed.

The final stage of the revolution took place almost immediately. The Provisional Government, which had assumed authority until a democratic parliamentary government could be convened, was overthrown by the Bolshevik wing of the Communist Party, led by Vladimir Lenin. Lenin's group was one of many socialist organizations that had been agitating to bring about fundamental changes in Russian society. Lenin favored a rigid discipline along socialist, but not necessarily democratic, lines. _____ (PLIC) in his plan for imposing the Communist philosophy on the country was his dictatorial role as Russia's leader. When he seized the reins of power, he moved quickly to consolidate his hold on the government, _____ (TORT) somewhat the goals of the socialist movement.

The Central Committee of the Communist Party, Lenin's group, quickly dominated the new government and moved to suppress all opposition. The civil war that followed with dissident elements of other socialist groups, as well as loyalists of the czar, was over quickly, and the revolution was accomplished.

1. The best title of this essay is
   A. The Role of the Communist Party in the Russian Revolution.
   B. The Failure of Czar Nicholas II.
   C. The Three Stages of the Russian Revolution.
   D. The Role of Lenin in the Russian Revolution.

2. The rule of Czar Nicholas II was followed by
   A. Communist rule.
   B. a provisional government.
   C. widespread disorder.
   D. increasing poverty.

3. According to the article, the first evidence that the czar would not accede to peasant demands was
   A. the rise of Communism.
   B. increased poverty.
   C. decreased autocratic government.
   D. the Winter Palace massacre.

4. Lenin, according to the author,
   A. went against the goals of his own party.
   B. subverted the decent goals of the Provisional Government.
   C. quickly ended Russian involvement in World War I.
   D. realized that fundamental changes in government were impossible.

Exercise VI. Drawing on your knowledge of roots and words in context, read the following selection and define the italicized words. If you cannot figure out the meaning of the words on your own, look them up in a dictionary. Note that *com* means "together."

The river *sinuates* around the margin of the game preserve, forming a rough natural boundary between the park and the surrounding residential area. Several years ago, local officials announced their intention to change the course of a large arc of the river in order to provide water power for the town's hydroelectric dam. The plan was halted, however, when several of the officials involved were found to be in *complicity* with owners of the electric utility in a scheme to embezzle millions. Investigators learned that the perpetrators had joined forces back when the preserve was first opened.

UNIT SEVENTEEN

SULT, ULT, SIL
Latin SALIRE, SULTUM, "to jump; to leap"

DESULTORY (de´ səl tôr ē) *adj.* moving or jumping from one thing to another
L. *de*, "from" + *sultum = leaping from place to place*
The candidate's *desultory* speech to the crowd failed to concisely deliver his message.
syn: disconnected

RESILIENT (ri zil´ yənt) *adj.* able to recover readily; persistent
L. *re*, "back" + *salire = leaping back*
The newborn proved *resilient* to the lethal virus and soon recovered fully.

EXULTANT (eks zul´ tənt) *adj.* marked by great joy or jubilation
L. *ex*, "out of" + *sultum = leaping out of*
Large crowds gathered along Broadway to welcome the *exultant* football team back from its victorious Super Bowl game.
syn: triumphant

The EXULTANT SULTAN jumped for joy.

PEND
Latin PENDERE, PENSUM, "to hang; to weigh"

EXPENDABLE (ek spen´ də bəl) *adj.* not necessary; dispensable
L. *ex*, "out of" + *pendere = able to be weighed out*
As part of the latest round of budget cuts, the governor fired all *expendable* personnel.

IMPENDING (im pend´ ing) *adj.* about to occur
L. *in*, "on" + *pendere = hanging on; hanging over*
All the faculty members awaited the *impending* retirement of the despised Dean.

APPEND (ə pend´) *v.* to add as a supplement; to attach
L. *ad*, "toward, onto" + *pendere = to hang something onto*
A list of corrections will be *appended* to the next edition of the book.

JECT
Latin JACERE, JECTUM, "to throw; to cast"

SUBJECTIVE (sub jək´ tiv) *adj.* varying according to personal opinion or
    perspective
L. *sub*, "under" + *jectum = throwing under*
While Jasmine felt that truth was unchanging and eternal, her sister claimed that
many truths were *subjective* and depended on circumstance and situation.
syn: personal   *ant: objective*

INTERJECT (in tər jekt´) *v.* to insert between other elements
L. *inter*, "between" + *jectum = to throw between*
Much to the surprise of the announcers, Connie *interjected* her opinion into the
argument regarding the golf tournament.
syn: interpose

UND
Latin UNDA, "wave"

UNDULATE (un´ dyə lāt) *v.* to move in a wavelike fashion; to ripple
The only way the snake could make its way to the top of the sand dune was to
undulate its body, almost hypnotically.

INUNDATE (in´ un dāt) *v.* to flood
L. *in*, "on, onto" + *unda = to flood*
After the radio first broadcast the song, people *inundated* the station with requests
to play it again.

REDOUND (rə downd´) *v.* to have an effect; to reflect
L. *re*, "back" + *unda = to flow back in waves*
No one was surprised that the story the egotistical head surgeon told *redounded* to
his own glory.

> The subject *of a sentence is the person who performs an action. Something that is* subjective *depends on a person's point of view. The opposite of* subjective *is objective.*

> *What, besides a snake, can you name that undulates?*

EXERCISES - UNIT SEVENTEEN

Exercise I. Complete the sentence in a way that shows you understand the meaning of the italicized vocabulary word.

1. Mrs. Wallace's kindergarten class was *exultant* at the thought of...

2. Francesca had a *resilient* personality; she was able to...

3. Darnell urged his friends to *inundate* the congressman with letters so that...

4. No food was considered *expendable* by the pioneer families because...

5. When the professor was criticized for being too *desultory* in his lectures, he said that...

6. The painter believed that interpretation of his masterpiece was *subjective* and...

7. When Pam told us of her *impending* marriage, we were surprised because...

8. Sandra saw the piece of fabric *undulate*, and she knew that...

9. Ziggy felt that he must *interject* his own opinion into...

10. The hard work that Cody had done in the yard *redounded* to...

11. An updated list of winners was *appended*...

Exercise II. Fill in the blank with the best word from the choices below. One word will not be used.

     undulate   interject   impending   expendable   exultant

1. Janelle should have been _____ on her wedding day, but she walked down the aisle in misery.

2. The wind coming ahead of a(n) _____ storm whipped the leaves and stray papers along the street.

3. From our seats at the top of the arena, the crowd seemed like a sea of _____ heads and arms.

4. The sergeant refused to believe that any of his soldiers were _____ in the battle.

Fill in the blank with the best word from the choices below. One word will not be used.

> append   inundate   desultory   subjective

5.   Lazy afternoons were perfect for _____ chats on all manner of subjects.

6.   Trish _____ a note of explanation to the back of her research paper.

7.   Opinions of the restaurant are necessarily _____, but it is a fact that the head chef has won numerous awards.

Fill in the blank with the best word from the choices below. One word will not be used.

> exultant   inundate   interject   resilient   redound

8.   When Janice launched into a speech about the lack of good drivers on the road, Kris _____ that she herself had received several traffic tickets.

9.   Because Mike was not a very _____ person, his friends wondered how he would survive the heartbreak of his breakup with Terry.

10.   Winds from the hurricane drew water from the ocean, which then _____ the coastal village.

11.   The leader of the rebel band swore that any cowardice would _____ to the dishonor of all the men fighting.

Exercise III. Choose the set of words that best completes the sentence.

1.   The professor allowed _____, off-subject conversations in his class, but would occasionally _____ a suggestion that got the students back on track.
      A. subjective; undulate
      B. desultory; interject
      C. impending; inundate
      D. expendable; undulate

2.   Kelly was so _____ that even when her coach told her she was a(n) _____ member of the team, she was only briefly upset.
      A. expendable; impending
      B. exultant; subjective
      C. desultory; impending
      D. resilient; expendable

3.   After the candidate's _____ victory speech on national television, she was _____ with requests for interviews.
      A. exultant; redounded
      B. expendable; appended
      C. resilient; desultory
      D. exultant; inundated

4.   The sailors believed that the violently _____ waters of the bay were a sign of a(n) _____ earthquake.
      A. impending; undulating
      B. subjective; expendable
      C. undulating; impending
      D. inundating; resilient

5.   Jim _____ a note to the report asking if some of the evidence was not more _____ than factual.
      A. inundated; expendable
      B. interjected; desultory
      C. appended; subjective
      D. undulated; exultant

Exercise IV. Complete the sentence by inferring information about the italicized word from its context.

1.   If Selma chooses to *append* a list of phone numbers to her memo, we will probably find the list…

2.   Kenny's face was probably *exultant* during the bicycle race because…

3.   Only the most *resilient* of the young medical students will be able to…

**Exercise V. Fill in each blank with the word from the Unit that best completes the sentence, using the root
      we supply as a clue. Then, answer the questions that follow the paragraphs.**

Although the United States had begun a space satellite program in 1955, the Soviet Union launched the world's first artificial satellite, Sputnik 1, on October 4, 1957. The Russians were _____ (ULT) to be the first in space, an achievement considered emblematic of Soviet scientific superiority, and the American public was equally dismayed by this undeniable accomplishment. Sputnik 1 was quickly followed on November 3 by Sputnik 2, which carried a dog into orbit. It was not until January 31, 1958, when the satellite Explorer was launched, that the American space program even began.

Another Soviet achievement actually resulted, indirectly, in an American on the moon. With the launch of Vostock I, carrying Yuri Gagarin, on April 12, 1961, the Soviets became the first to send a man into space. The United States was galvanized by the event, and John F. Kennedy committed the nation to placing a man on the moon before the end of the 1960s. While a series of Lunar Orbiter vehicles explored the surface of the moon, tests of manned flight vehicles were carried out. Research had to be suspended after a tragic fire killed the first three moon-bound astronauts, but it was soon resumed. On December 21, 1968, with the launch of Apollo 8, the first humans were carried into orbit around the moon.

On July 20, 1969, Apollo 11 placed humans on the moon's surface for the first time.

By December 1972, when the lunar program ended, research into living and working conditions in space had been underway for several years. Orbiting space labs (Skylab for the United States, Soyuz for the Soviet Union) provided an environment in which astronauts could study these conditions. When astronauts from the Apollo 18 spacecraft and the Russian Soyuz 19 linked up, a program of cooperation had finally begun.

In 1976, the United States space shuttle *Explorer*, the first of its kind, debuted. Unlike previous vehicles, space shuttles could go into orbit, return to Earth, and be reused to transport crew and material to space labs. Major setbacks still occurred: on January 28, 1986, the shuttle *Challenger* exploded upon launching, killing all seven of its crew members, and on February 1, 2003, the shuttle *Columbia* broke apart upon re-entry, killing its crew of seven. Debate over the wisdom of sending humans into space was ignited after each of these tragedies, but the program proved _____ (SIL), and plans for building and launching shuttles resumed.

1.   The best title for this essay would be
       A.   Putting a Man on the Moon.
       B.   The Space Race Ends.
       C.   Milestones in Space Exploration.
       D.   The Debate on Humans in Space.

2.   The race to put a man on the moon essentially began with
       A.   President Kennedy's 1961 speech.
       B.   the American satellite program in 1955.
       C.   the orbital flight of Yuri Gagarin in 1961.
       D.   the Apollo program.

3.   Before shuttles, space vehicles
       A.   cost a great deal of money.
       B.   were dangerous for human beings.
       C.   could be used more than once.
       D.   were not able to be reused.

4.   Sputnik 1, according to the author,
       A.   was a problem that needed to be solved.
       B.   worried the United States.
       C.   led to a man on the moon.
       D.   was of concern to the entire world.

Exercise VI. Drawing on your knowledge of roots and words in context, read the following selection and define the italicized words. If you cannot figure out the meaning of the words on your own, look them up in a dictionary. Note that *dis* means "apart."

   In early spring, some of the trees in the orchard release *dissilient* seed pods, which can be collected and sold for their nutritious inner hulls. They must be gathered promptly, however, for as soon as the pod bursts, the nutrients in the seeds begin to break down. Other trees drape their *pendulous* fruit over the fences on the edge of the orchard. Some of the apples and pears hang so low that passing schoolchildren can reach up and pick them.

UNIT EIGHTEEN

SEM
Latin SEMEN, SEMINIS, "seed"
Latin SEMINARE, SEMINATUM, "to sow"

DISSEMINATE   (di sem´ ə nāt)   v.   to scatter; to spread
L. *dis*, "apart" + *seminatum* = *to sow apart; to sow widely*
The candidate hired a staff of three to help her *disseminate* her campaign information to the community.
syn: circulate   ant: withhold

SEMINAL   (sem´ ə nəl)   adj.   fundamentally influential; important
The Big Bang theory was *seminal* in the quest to discover the creation of the universe.
                                    ant: inconsequential

The SEMINAL book on CRIMINAL justice

FLOR
Latin FLOS, FLORIS, "flower"

FLORID   (flô´ rid)   adj.   overly decorated; showy
The dull, plain lines of the painting reflected an artistic backlash against the *florid*, busy patterns of an earlier movement.
syn: flowery   ant: plain

FLOURISH   (flûr´ ish)   v.   to thrive; to prosper
The new railroad station will help the town's economy *flourish*.
                                    ant: die

⚑ *Plants use innumerable techniques to disseminate seeds: burrs, wind, birds, insects, humans, etc. Some plants, however, have exploding pods that can shoot seeds nearly 300 feet for dissemination. Amazingly, the largest seed on the planet, which is a coconut, weighs over 3 pounds; it floats on water in order to root in another place.*

⚑ *Have you ever heard that someone finished something "with a flourish"? The noun flourish means "something extra added for style," like the wave of the hand a magician gives at the end of a trick.*

RAD
Latin RADIX, RADICIS, "root"

DERACINATE (də raˊ sə nāt) *v.* to uproot; to remove from one's homeland
The Great Potato Famine of the 1850s *deracinated* many Irish families and forced them to come to America.

IRRADICABLE (i radˊ i kə bəl) *adj.* impossible to destroy
L. *in*, "not" + *radicis* = *not able to be uprooted*
The insect population in our attic proved *irradicable*, so we gave up trying to exterminate them and hired a professional.
syn: deep-rooted

ERADICATE (i radˊ i kāt) *v.* to destroy; to get rid of
L. *ex*, "out of" + *radicis* = *to pull out of by the roots*
The army was called in to *eradicate* the dangerous species of huge rats that had begun nesting on the island.
syn: abolish, eliminate

GERM
Latin GERMINARE, GERMINATUM, "to sprout; to grow"

GERMINATE (jərˊ mə nāt) *v.* to cause to grow
We planted the seeds in dirt inside egg cartons first to help them *germinate* more quickly.

GERMINAL (jərˊ mə nəl) *adj.* occurring in the earliest stage of development
Dr. Jenkins was active during the *germinal* stages of Canada's space program, but retired before the first launch.

GERMANE (jər mānˊ) *adj.* related to a subject or topic; relevant
A working knowledge of Spanish is *germane* to the position at the Latin American Cultural Center in downtown Cleveland.
syn: pertinent

▥ Deracinate *comes from the French word for "root,"* racine; *in turn,* racine *comes from* radicina, *a form of* radix.

▥ *You may have heard of someone having "the germ of an idea" and thought it might be related to a* germ *that causes disease, but, as you can see from its Latin origin, the phrase means something that can sprout and grow in the mind.*

EXERCISES – UNIT EIGHTEEN

Exercise I. Complete the sentence in a way that shows you understand the meaning of the italicized vocabulary word.

1. Because she was the originator of some of the most *seminal* ideas in environmental science, Rachel was known as…

2. Mike's design scheme for the new computer was given time to *germinate*, so he…

3. Kevin reacted to the author's *florid* style by…

4. Whenever a journalist asked a question that was not *germane*, the presidential spokesman…

5. Entire families in the rural county were *deracinated* by…

6. Knowing that his client's novel was only in a *germinal* state, the author's agent…

7. In an attempt to *eradicate* deer in the Huntingville area, the city council…

8. In order to *disseminate* the church's ideas, the minister…

9. The sergeant worried that the problem of rebellion in his unit was *irradicable* because…

10. Tina *flourished* in her new fourth-grade classroom as she…

Exercise II. Fill in the blank with the best word from the choices below. One word will not be used.

deracinate	seminal	flourish	germane

1. The composer's _____ work was vastly influential for over two hundred years.

2. The current economic crisis is threatening to permanently _____ many poor families from the land they have farmed for centuries.

3. The detective dismissed many of the calls received on the tip line as not _____ to the case.

Fill in the blank with the best word from the choices below. One word will not be used.

germinate   disseminate   flourish   germinal

4.   The delicate orchids, which could _____ in the warm, humid beach home, failed to thrive in our chilly city apartment.

5.   Young fans of the baseball team volunteered to _____ information about the upcoming games in the surrounding towns.

6.   The computer science program at the university is only in its _____ stage, but in a few years, it should be one of the largest in the country.

Fill in the blank with the best word from the choices below. One word will not be used.

irradicable   florid   disseminate   eradicate   germinate

7.   Looking to _____ malaria in equatorial populations, the doctors studied the transmission and life cycle of the disease.

8.   Do you think most romances are spontaneous, or do they _____ over a long period of time?

9.   A strong superstitious streak seemed to be _____ in my grandmother; no matter what we said, she would never walk down 13th Avenue.

10.   I was never a fan of that _____ decorative style, which involved elaborately carved furniture and an overabundance of fabric and gilt paint.

Exercise III. Choose the set of words that best completes the sentence.

1.   Doctor Pierre's ideas on nutrition were _____, helping to _____ malnutrition in his home country.
      A. florid; germinate
      B. florid; flourish
      C. seminal; eradicate
      D. germinal; flourish

2.   Though his family had been _____ from the old country, Franz's business was _____ in America.
      A. flourished; irradicable
      B. deracinated; flourishing
      C. eradicated; germinal
      D. disseminated; germane

3.   Once the scientist had _____ her findings in the research community, new ideas for the data began to _____ in the minds of many scholars.
     A.   disseminated; germinate
     B.   deracinated; eradicate
     C.   flourished; eradicate
     D.   deracinated; flourish

4.   Though the revolution was only in a(n) _____ stage, the government feared it would grow into a(n) _____ plague of rebellion.
     A.   seminal; germinal
     B.   germane; florid
     C.   germinal; irradicable
     D.   irradicable; florid

5.   Not only is the author's style _____ and melodramatic, but he also spends too much time on topics that are not _____ to his original subject.
     A.   florid; germane
     B.   irradicable; germinal
     C.   seminal; florid
     D.   germinal; seminal

Exercise IV. Complete the sentence by inferring information about the italicized word from its context.

1.   If a musical composition is in a *germinal* state, it can probably be found…

2.   In order to *disseminate* news about an upcoming political debate, campaign volunteers may…

3.   If a family fears that it may be *deracinated*, it may be because…

Exercise V. Fill in each blank with the word from the Unit that best completes the sentence, using the root we supply as a clue. Then, answer the questions that follow the paragraphs.

Although rain forests are popularly thought of as _____ (FLOR) only in the Amazon region of South America and in equatorial Africa, they actually extend around the globe in a green belt at the equator. Almost half the world's rain forests grow in the Americas, but others are found in Asia, Africa, and even on Pacific islands and parts of Australia. This belt of green around the globe contains a wide variety of plant and animal species that benefit humanity in many significant ways. For many people, the primary value of these areas is economic. They produce wood for fuel, as well as timber, having a value of billions of dollars a year. Other products include plant fibers, resins, oils, fruits, and nuts. The beauty of these areas also attracts many tourists, providing substantial contributions to the economies of the nations where the forests are located.

However, rain forests also have significant environmental and scientific value. They play a vital role in the earth's ecosystem because they absorb enormous quantities of rain, which then return to the atmosphere as water vapor from plant photosynthesis. This process helps to control temperature in the forests, as well as in other regions of the earth. Absorbing light and heat, as well as massive amounts of carbon dioxide, these vast regions help keep global temperatures relatively constant.

In addition to playing a _____ (SEM) role in the global ecosystem, rain forests constitute a unique ecosystem in themselves. They have generated increasing scientific interest in the interplay of the enormous diversity of life they contain—a diversity that has scarcely begun to be explored.

Unfortunately, the environmental and scientific value of the rain forests has been overshadowed by their economic potential. This use has led the populations of the countries where they are located to _____ (RAD) over half these forests in the past fifty years through logging, farming (particularly of the slash-and-burn type), mining, and other activities that result in the clearing of large areas of forest. Most of these nations are regions of great poverty and population increase, and under enormous pressure to exploit the forests for short-term economic benefit. Once forest areas are cleared, they are rarely reforested. As scientists around the world have come to appreciate the negative global impact of deforestation and _____ (SEM) a sense of alarm about it, many governments and conservation groups have taken steps to stem the practice and even reverse its effects. However, the destruction still continues at an alarming rate, and much remains to be done.

1. The primary value of rain forests, according to the article, is
   A. economic.
   B. as a source of raw materials.
   C. environmental and scientific.
   D. related to their diversity.

2. Rain forests are located
   A. in every country.
   B. near the equator.
   C. in poor countries.
   D. primarily in accessible areas.

3. Scientific interest in rain forests
   A. is relatively recent.
   B. has led to better use of them.
   C. is centered on the animals they contain.
   D. has focused on their role in the ecosystem.

4. The clearing of the rain forests
   A. has taken place for only fifty years.
   B. is necessary for poor nations.
   C. has attracted many tourists.
   D. is cause for increasing scientific concern.

5. The author of the passage would probably disagree with which statement?
   A. People are primarily responsible for what is happening to the climate.
   B. The climate will probably be fine, even without humans altering their behavior.
   C. Rising sea levels will probably cause drastic changes to our way of life.
   D. Scientists have differing, but valid, opinions about global climate change.

Exercise VI. Drawing on your knowledge of roots and words in context, read the following selection and define the italicized words. If you cannot figure out the meaning of the words on your own, look them up in a dictionary. Note that *ef*, from *ex*, means "out from."

The ancient *seminary* stands atop a bluff overlooking miles of scrub brush and desert. Here, unformed young novices and wise men at the *efflorescence* of their knowledge studied and debated the future of their religious path. Each had discovered within himself the seed of some yearning to know his Creator and had dedicated himself to the tending of this desire. Though some lost their calling in a few months or a year, an amazing number became true contributors to the body of theological study.

UNIT NINETEEN

DECOR
Latin DÉCOR, "beauty; appropriateness; order"

DECORUM (də kôr´ əm) *n.* an appropriateness of behavior or conduct
Bernadette was careful to exhibit the utmost *decorum* during her visit with her stern grandparents.
syn: propriety

DECOROUS (dek´ ər əs) *adj.* proper; mannerly
All the guests were expected to exhibit *decorous* behavior at all times.

The DECOROUS Duchess never Drank DAIQUIRIS.

ORN
Latin ORNARE, ORNATUM, "to embellish; to decorate; to equip"

ADORN (ə dôrn´) *v.* to decorate; to heighten the beauty of
L. *ad*, "toward, onto" + *ornatum* = *hung decorations on*
Thirty-three gold statues *adorned* the birthday cake of the award-winning director of the movie.

SUBORN (sə bôrn´) *v.* to convince someone to lie or commit a crime
L. *sub*, "beneath" + *ornare* = *to equip beneath; to equip secretly*
The attorney was found to be in contempt of court for trying to *suborn* the defendant's mother.
syn: coerce

ORNATE (ôr nāt´) *adj.* heavily decorated; intricate
The *ornate* chandelier gave the dining hall an added touch of beauty and class.
syn: florid   *ant: plain*

Ⅲ *Without proper decorum, Congress would be noisy, filled with insults, and nothing would get done, just as it is with proper decorum. —Anonymous*

Ⅲ *Ornaments are decorations that enhance the appearance of one's environment, especially on holidays. If something is ornamental, it is primarily decorative rather than functional.*

FORM
Latin FORMA, "form; order"

FORMULAIC (fôrm ū lā´ ək) *adj.* done according to an overused method; trite
Critics expecting a *formulaic* reworking of the same old drama will be pleasantly
surprised by the acting in the new Hollywood film.
syn: clichéd   *ant: original*

FORMALITY (fôrm al´ ə tē) *n.* something done only for show or ceremony
Because my client and I know one another so well, we have dispensed with the
formality of shaking hands.

FORMULATE (fôrm´ ū lāt) *v.* to come up with; to devise
Bonnie *formulated* a plan whereby she would receive ten percent of the money her
sister made.

ORD
Latin ORDINARE, ORDINATUM, "to organize; to put in order"

INORDINATE (in ôrd´ ə nət) *adj.* too abundant; excessive
L. *in*, "not" + *ordinatum* = *not in order; not limited*
If the birthday party was indeed "enjoyed by all," why was there an *inordinate*
amount of sobbing going on there?
syn: superfluous   *ant: dearth, absence*

ORDAIN (ôr dān´) *v.* to formally order; to command
The king's minister declined to question anything the king had *ordained.*

PREORDAINED (prē ôr dānd´) *adj.* determined in advance
L. *pre*, "before" + *ordinare* = *ordered before*
Danny hoped that he would win the track meet but did not believe that his
success was *preordained.*

> ▥ *Besides formulating a plan, a judgment, an argument, or a recipe, what other objects can you put after* formulate?

> ▥ *To ordain can mean "to invest with holy authority," as well as simply "to order." Thus, a minister or priest is* ordained *before he or she can conduct a service.*

EXERCISES - UNIT NINETEEN

Exercise I. Complete the sentence in a way that shows you understand the meaning of the italicized vocabulary word.

1.   Each team tried to make its parade float as *ornate* as possible so that…

2.   The nuns always exhibited perfect *decorum* in…

3.   On the anniversary of the school's founding, the main classroom building was *adorned* with…

4.   Because giving gifts on birthdays is a *formality* in our office, some have said we should…

5.   The admiral believed that his loss of the naval battle was *preordained* because…

6.   In a letter to his employer, Billy claimed he had to do an *inordinate* amount of…

7.   Adam stated that he had been *suborned* by his wife and urged that…

8.   Deborah was to conduct the ceremony in a *decorous* manner because…

9.   The creative writing teacher tried to steer his students away from *formulaic* plots because…

10.   After a fire destroyed three-fourths of the city, the mayor *ordained* that…

11.   Trying to *formulate* the answer to the cause of the explosion, the team of scientists…

Exercise II. Fill in the blank with the best word from the choices below. One word will not be used.

preordained   formulaic   ornate   decorum

1.   The _____ setting of the diamond consisted of several complex knots of gold and rubies.

2.   It is important to dress appropriately and exhibit _____ when representing your school at an academic event.

3.   The audience was composed entirely of people hostile to one contestant; therefore, the outcome of the show was _____.

Fill in the blank with the best word from the choices below. One word will not be used.

        decorous   adorn   formulaic   inordinate   suborn

4.   One of the larger oil companies was accused of trying to _____ a local congressman.

5.   Vanessa's _____ behavior at the banquet gained her a reputation as a graceful and polite girl.

6.   When the comedian's routine began to seem _____ and tired, audiences stopped coming to his shows.

7.   The collar of the dress was _____ with tiny purple and white flowers.

Fill in the blank with the best word from the choices below. One word will not be used.

        formulate   ordain   decorous   formality   inordinate

8.   After much debate, the company _____ a policy to deal with inter-office conflicts.

9.   Dean complained that his nightly homework seemed to require a(n) _____ amount of his time.

10.   The editors of the magazine have _____ that, every year, some lucky movie star will be named the "Celebrity of the Year."

11.   Because the law would go into effect regardless, the signature of the vice president on the bill was a mere _____.

Exercise III. Choose the set of words that best completes the sentence.

1.   Linda usually believed that using the proper fork was essential for maintaining _____, but it seemed like a ridiculous _____ at a barbecue.
     A. decorum; formality
     B. adornment; decorum
     C. ornateness; adornment
     D. formality; adornment

2.   The _____ choreography of the skating team involved many leaps and spins, but not a(n) _____ number.
     A. formulaic; decorous
     B. ornate; inordinate
     C. inordinate; ornate
     D. preordained; formulaic

3.   We could tell by Chris's evil grin that he was _____ a plan to _____ his innocent friend.
     A.   ordaining; formulate
     B.   suborning; adorn
     C.   formulating; suborn
     D.   adorning; formulate

4.   Though the novel is _____ with some glorious touches, its plot is fundamentally _____ and conventional.
     A.   formulated; ornate
     B.   ordained; decorous
     C.   adorned; formulaic
     D.   suborned; inordinate

5.   Mother _____ that until my aunt and uncle left our home, our behavior would be far more _____ than usual.
     A.   suborned; formulaic
     B.   ordained; decorous
     C.   formulated; inordinate
     D.   adorned; decorous

Exercise IV. Complete the sentence by inferring information about the italicized word from its context.

1.   In order to *suborn* his boss at the power plant, Lowell may do something like…

2.   When chores are *preordained* by your parents, you probably…

3.   If cleaning out her storage locker requires an *inordinate* amount of work, Danielle may…

Exercise V. Fill in each blank with the word from the Unit that best completes the sentence, using the root we supply as a clue. Then, answer the questions that follow the paragraphs.

Most of us yearn for a glimpse of high society. We imagine a life of luxury and ease. Of course, most of us must also rely on stereotypes, media representations, and our imagination to know what it is truly like to live in high society. Only a tiny percent of the population can afford to indulge its desire for such a lifestyle.

However, when we imagine high society, we consider more than riches. Naturally, some currency must be a prerequisite for this lifestyle, but money alone does not create a life of luxury. A wealthy individual could manage a sheep ranch in Wyoming or, like Saint Katherine Drexel, retreat from the upper crust into which she was born and use her wealth to educate society's outcasts.

When we speak of the high life to which we aspire, we envision all that represents breeding and culture, all that appeals to a sense of luxury and pleasure. We first picture the home: an estate in a picturesque setting. There is that special solitude and peace that comes from dwelling in the center of acres of land, lawns, woods, gardens, and maybe even a pond. Yet, there is simultaneously the comfort and laughter of friends. In a home as large as an estate, entertaining can be effortlessly gracious. The spaciousness is comfortable and just the right décor lends an air of conviviality to the rooms. Indoors and out, there is a sense of welcome and ease. And, of course, this effect is facilitated by the caterers who manage the event. How wonderful to be a host free to mingle without the onus of setup and clean up!

In addition to the estate, the members of high society that we imagine must reflect good taste in all they do. They interact with others in a _____ (DECOR) manner, ever polite and appropriate. They pursue activities indicative of their status, culture, and standing. Perhaps members of high society collect art, maintain and ride horses, furnish their homes with period pieces, support the arts by attending theatrical and musical performances, and _____ (ORN) themselves in designer originals.

In the 20th century, one individual epitomized high culture and society—Jacqueline Kennedy Onassis. As a society, we have admired and emulated her. Her very being represented refinement and good taste. She fulfilled our wish to live the high life. She was an equestrian, First Lady, interior decorator, talented editor, and an individual of impeccable bearing. More than her wealth, and all that it bought, however, the people of the United States admired her grace. This is what made all that we knew of her seem so magnificent, and this, fortunately, can be had for free.

1.   Which sentence states the main point of the article?
     A.   Money alone does not create high society.
     B.   Only a few people can afford a life in high society.
     C.   Jacqueline Kennedy Onassis epitomized high culture and society.
     D.   Wealthy people live in estates.

2.   The best title for this article is
     A.   A Glimpse of High Society.
     B.   A Life of Luxury and Ease.
     C.   Jacqueline Kennedy Onassis.
     D.   It Takes Wealth.

3.   The last paragraph
     A.   explains Jacqueline Kennedy Onassis's exemplary grace.
     B.   indicates that wealthy people have many possibilities in life.
     C.   contradicts the typical view of Jacqueline Kennedy Onassis.
     D.   proves the arguments stated in the rest of the article.

Exercise VI. Drawing on your knowledge of roots and words in context, read the following selection and define the italicized words. If you cannot figure out the meaning of the words on your own, look them up in a dictionary. Note that *con* means "with."

Though she was usually *conformable* to the requests made by City Hall, Fire Chief Melissa Lee put up some resistance to the latest official demand. The new *ordinance* against noise pollution required that she lower the volume of the sirens on her trucks. At last month's town meeting, Chief Lee explained that the sirens had been effectively warning traffic to move out of the way of emergency vehicles for years. She warned that the new regulation could result in injury or death if the fire personnel arrived at their destination too late.

UNIT TWENTY

MUN

Latin MUNUS, MUNERIS, "payment; gift; resource; public work"
Latin COMMUNIS, "common"

MUNIFICENT   (myōō nif´ i sənt)   *adj.*   generous; giving
L. *munus*, "gift" + *facere*, "to make" = *making many gifts*
Phil was *munificent* in his donation of three million dollars to AIDS research.
ant: stingy

REMUNERATE   (rē myōōn´ ə rāt)   *v.*   to compensate; to pay
L. *re*, "back" + *muneris* = *to give gifts back*
The city council was unable to think of a way to properly *remunerate* Ted for his effort at fighting crime.

COMMUNAL   (kə mū´ nəl)   *adj.*   shared by the people of a community; public
The *communal* bathrooms in the dorms took some time for Joan to get used to.

EXCOMMUNICATE   (eks kə mū´ ni kāt)   *v.*   to exclude from membership in
   a group
The archbishop will *excommunicate* the king for his crimes against the Church.

INCOMMUNICADO   (in kə mū ni kä´ dō)   *adj.*   unable or not allowed to
   communicate with others
Agent Riley will be *incommunicado* until the danger in the capital has passed.

PREC, PRAIS

Latin PRETIUM, "price"
Latin PRETIARE, PRETIATUM, "to price; to appraise; to value"

APPRECIABLE   (ə prē´ shə bəl)   *adj.*   able to be measured or perceived
L. *ad*, "toward" + *pretiare* = *able to be valued*
If the two diamonds had no *appreciable* differences, why was one so much more expensive?

APPRAISE   (ə prāz´)   *v.*   to evaluate; to estimate the quality, amount, size, and
   other features of
L. *ad*, "toward" + *pretium* = *to give a price toward*
In order to get an accurate insurance rate quote, the Daniels family had to have their home *appraised* by the bank.

Ⅲ *A* munus *was a gift, often a public building or spectacle, given to the Roman public by a local official. The words* common *and* communal *(*com*, "together, jointly" +* munis*) describe such a gift and mean "held by the people jointly." To* communicate *is to exchange ideas or words that you hold in* common *with others.*

Ⅲ *Do not confuse* appraise, *"to estimate the value of," with* apprise, *"to explain or tell," which is frequently followed with the word* of, *as in, "I was* apprised *of my college acceptance in an email."*

MERIT, MERE
Latin MERERE, MERITUM, "to earn; to deserve"

MERITORIOUS   (mer i tôr´ ē əs)   *adj.*   deserving reward or praise
The graduate's *meritorious* work earned him an award for excellence.

DEMERIT   (dē mə´ rit)   *n.*   a fault or flaw
L. *de*, "down" + *meritum* = *down in merit; reduced in merit*
Calvin said that the poor service he had received at the car dealership was
certainly a *demerit* he would mention in his evaluation.

MERETRICIOUS   (mer i trish´ əs)   *adj.*   seemingly true, but actually false
No article as full of *meretricious* arguments as Dr. Brannigan's would be published
by any respectable science journal.
syn: specious

*MARY'S MERETRICIOUS behavior
did not MERIT TRICIA'S approval.*

▥ *Most soldiers who receive the country's highest military award, the Congressional Medal of Honor, given for their meritorious service in trying to save others' lives, believe that any soldier would have done exactly the same thing they did. Service to one's country is the honor they seek; the Medal of Honor recognizes service "above and beyond" the call of duty. Fewer than 3,500 Medals of Honor have been given—out of the millions of people who have served—in the history of the United States.*

▥ *Though meretricious sounds like merit, it is actually a negative term. In ancient Rome, a meretrix was a prostitute, someone who earned (merere) her living. Something meretricious is attractive and flashy, but actually worth little.*

EXERCISES - UNIT TWENTY

Exercise I. Complete the sentence in a way that shows you understand the meaning of the italicized vocabulary word.

1.   The lottery winner was not *munificent* with his new winnings because…

2.   The councilwoman's years of *meritorious* behavior earned her…

3.   Mother warned that patience could be a *demerit* when it came to things like…

4.   The CEO worried that if he did not *remunerate* his remaining employees…

5.   The dancer claimed that the new book about his life was *meretricious* because…

6.   Though the park was legally a *communal* spot, Meredith found that…

7.   Jordan decided to have his sister *appraise* the car he was thinking of buying because…

8.   Because Hiram has been *incommunicado* for so long, we have all begun to assume that…

9.   There was an *appreciable* change in the mood on the island when…

10.   In an overly formal way, the person in charge announced, "Niles, you are hereby and forever *excommunicated* from the poker game because…

Exercise II. Fill in the blank with the best word from the choices below. One word will not be used.

communal	meretricious	remunerate	appreciable	demerit

1.   Trina denounced the professor's thesis as the most _____ sort of argument.

2.   The special delegation of citizens voted to use the extra _____ funds to build a new school.

3.   When asked to honestly discuss any _____ in her personality, Chelsea mentioned disorganization and stubbornness.

4.   The babysitter promised to _____ the child's family for any damage done to the house during her sitting hours.

Fill in the blank with the best word from the choices below. One word will not be used.

   meritorious   munificent   appraise   appreciable

5.   Brian promised that if he were successful on the quiz show, he would be as _____ as his bank account allowed.

6.   The commencement speaker praised the young graduates of the police academy for their _____ conduct during their training.

7.   The rainstorm lowered the temperature a(n) _____ amount.

Fill in the blank with the best word from the choices below. One word will not be used.

   excommunicate   appraise   incommunicado   munificent

8.   The author apologized to his friends for being _____, saying he had been hard at work on his latest novel.

9.   The children's fights never lasted long; anyone _____ from the group was welcomed back an hour later.

10. Doug claimed that his car had been _____ and is now valued at $100,000 by several automobile experts.

Exercise III. Choose the set of words that best completes the sentence.

1.   Though the priest argued that he was guilty of no _____, he was eventually _____ from the Church.
     A. excommunication; appraised
     B. demerit; excommunicated
     C. demerit; remunerated
     D. remuneration; appraised

2.   A special legal commission was called into session to _____ and evaluate the standards for development of _____ areas like parks and jogging paths.
     A. remunerate; munificent
     B. excommunicate; appreciable
     C. appraise; communal
     D. excommunicate; meretricious

3.   Employees who believed their _____ conduct would be _____ by the company were in for a rude disappointment.
     A. munificent; excommunicated
     B. meritorious; remunerated
     C. communal; appraised
     D. appreciable; remunerated

4.   Though Tom had a reputation as a(n) _____ patron of struggling artists, the money he donated did not
      make a(n) _____ difference in their lives.
      A. appreciable; communal
      B. meritorious; munificent
      C. incommunicado; meritorious
      D. munificent; appreciable

5.   The defendant claimed that he had been _____ because he was in prison for several months on a(n)
      _____ and invalid charge.
      A. munificent; incommunicado
      B. incommunicado; meretricious
      C. appreciable; meritorious
      D. communal; appreciable

Exercise IV. Complete the sentence by inferring information about the italicized word from its context.

1.   If the children consider Lloyd their most *munificent* uncle, it is probably because he does things like…

2.   Althea's *meritorious* behavior may result in her being…

3.   If the difference in taste between two kinds of soda is not *appreciable*, a person choosing between the two
      will probably…

**Exercise V. Fill in each blank with the word from the Unit that best completes the sentence, using the root
      we supply as a clue. Then, answer the questions that follow the paragraphs.**

Thousands of Americans are currently incarcerated in "supermax" prisons. Designed to curtail prisoner-on-prisoner and prisoner-on-guard violence, these high-tech prisons have given birth to a less visible, but no less harmful, form of violence: psychological torture.

There is no _____ (PREC) difference between being confined in a supermax prison and being forced to spend one's entire prison term in "the hole." Supermax prisoners spend twenty-three hours per day in solitary, windowless cells sealed with steel doors. Interaction with fellow prisoners is all but impossible, as supermaxes do away with any _____ (MUN) recreation spaces or lounges. Instead, each prisoner is able to exercise only a few times a week in a small, enclosed space. Contact with guards is limited to the time it takes to lead a shackled prisoner to and from this recreation space; meals are slid to inmates through slots in their steel cell doors. Inmates essentially spend their entire lives _____ (MUN).

Such aggressive isolation takes a dramatic toll on the mental health of supermax inmates. The prolonged lack of social interaction and mental stimuli causes many prisoners to develop depression, acute anxiety, or psychosis.

Claustrophobia, hallucinations, and an impaired ability to think or concentrate are not uncommon. One study by the Washington State Department of Corrections revealed that nearly 30% of that state's supermax inmates display symptoms of serious psychiatric disorders, which is more than twice the rate of the nation's prison population overall. Few supermaxes are equipped to offer inmates the mental health care such disorders necessitate.

The asocial supermax atmosphere leaves no room for the possibility of rehabilitation. Originally intended to hold only criminals considered "the worst of the worst," supermaxes are increasingly becoming filled with nonviolent offenders for whom room cannot be found at less extreme facilities. When released, these prisoners will find it all the more difficult to rejoin society and function as responsible citizens.

Of course, many citizens look at the infamous prisoners currently or formerly in supermax prisons—the Unabomber, the Oklahoma City bombers, gang leaders, the Boston Marathon bomber, men involved in 9/11, Mafia bosses, drug kingpins, white supremacists, and spies—and decide that these people should continue to pay for their horrible crimes and should never be released.

1.   Which of the following would be the best title for the passage?
     A. Supermax and Psychological Cruelty
     B. Supermaxes: Not Just for the Violent
     C. The Best for the Worst
     D. You Can Help Make Supermaxes Illegal

2.   Nonviolent prisoners end up in supermaxes because
     A. all who break the law are treated equally.
     B. they are frequently insane.
     C. they make the overall supermax population less violent.
     D. they cannot be accommodated elsewhere.

3.   A study by the Washington State Department of Corrections found that compared with the general prison
     population, Washington's supermax prisoners are
     A. twice as likely to die in prison.
     B. twice as likely to develop mental health problems.
     C. two times more isolated.
     D. twice as likely to cause trouble when they re-enter society.

4.   The article mentions that supermaxes do not have
     A. cafeterias.
     B. communal recreation spaces.
     C. libraries.
     D. prison yards.

**Exercise VI. Drawing on your knowledge of roots and words in context, read the following selection and
     define the italicized words. If you cannot figure out the meaning of the words on your own, look
     them up in a dictionary. Note that *de* means "down" and *e*, from *ex*, means "out from; from."**

The peso, Mexico's official unit of currency, has *depreciated* to about ten percent of the American dollar. The
drop in value comes on the heels of tough economic times and was worsened by the recent worldwide recession.
Dr. Lee Ramirez, Professor *Emeritus* of Latin American Studies at Copen State University, expects the currency to
rebound as the global political situation stabilizes, but warns that a difficult road is still ahead for the Mexican
economy.

UNIT TWENTY-ONE

STILL
Latin STILLARE, STILLATUM, "drip"

INSTILL   (in stil´)   *v.*   to gradually put into
L. *in*, "in" + *stilla* = *to drip into*
George's parents tried hard to *instill* traditional virtues into their son.
syn: imbue, impart

DISTILL   (di stil´)   *v.*   to extract the essence of
L. *de*, "down" + *stillare* = *to drip down*
Phon's summary *distilled* the high points of the movie.

LU
Latin LUERE, LUTUM, "to wash"

ABLUTION   (ə blū´ shən)   *n.*   a cleansing, especially religious or spiritual
L. *ab*, "away" + *luere* = *wash away*
Considering himself a sinner, George went in search of *ablution*.
syn: purification

ALLUVIAL   (ə lū´ vē əl)   *adj.*   deposited by a stream
L. *ad*, "toward" + *luere* = *wash toward*
The *alluvial* soil turned out to be rich in gold and other valuable materials.

LAC
Latin LACRIMA, "tear"

LACHRYMAL   (la´ krə məl)   *adj.*   having to do with tears
The smoke irritated my *lachrymal* glands, causing me to tear up even though I was not sad.

LACHRYMOSE   (la´ krə mōs)   *adj.*   teary; oversentimental
The soap opera was full of *lachrymose* death scenes and syrupy love stories.
syn: weepy

Distill can be abstract or concrete. One can distill perfume or alcohol by separating them from other substances; a long essay boiled down into a brief summary is also a distillation.

The suffix –ose means "full of," while the suffix –al means "relating to."

LAV
Latin LAVERE, "to wash"

LAVISH (la´ vish) *adj.* 1. luxuriously abundant; extravagant
v. 2. to give in abundance; to heap
1. A *lavish* display of toys made children looking into the window jump with excitement.
2. Aunt Mildred *lavished* presents on her ungrateful nephew.

RIPA
Latin RIPA, "stream"

RIPARIAN (rə´ per ē ən) *adj.* having to do with the banks of a body of water
The fishermen argued with their government over who had *riparian* rights.

MEANDER
Greek MAIANDROS, god of the Meander River

MEANDER (mē´ an dər) *v.* to wander; to move without direction
On the day of the fair, I could look out my window and see my neighbors *meandering* through the streets.

The stray dog MEANDERED over to ME AND HER.

FLU, FLUCT
Latin FLUERE, FLUCTUS, "to flow"

FLUENT (flū´ ənt) *adj.* 1. able to speak smoothly
2. smooth; graceful
1. Most of the employees of the company were *fluent* in Spanish, as well as English.
2. Lisa's *fluent* verse won her awards in several poetry contests.

FLUCTUATE (flək´ chə wāt) *v.* to change irregularly
The amount of sodium in the water *fluctuates* with daily accumulated rainfall.

The gratification of wealth is not found in mere possession or in lavish expenditure, but in its wise application.
—Miguel de Cervantes, author of Don Quixote

A flume is a channel through which water is forced in order to carry logs or other heavy objects. The word flume is from the Latin flumen, "river," which is derived from fluere.

EXERCISES - UNIT TWENTY-ONE

Exercise I. Complete the sentence in a way that shows you understand the meaning of the italicized vocabulary word.

1.   No matter how the stock market *fluctuates*,...

2.   The soldiers were told not to *meander* because...

3.   Scientists tested the *alluvial* material in order to...

4.   When talking to the new recruits, the general tried to *instill*...

5.   The singer's *fluent* phrasing was a result of...

6.   Alex *lavished* his girlfriend with...

7.   Kenny hoped that a *lachrymose* speech might convince his teacher to...

8.   An artificial *lachrymal* system may allow the robot to...

9.   The Native American healer said a prayer of *ablution* in order to...

10. The purpose of the conference was to discuss *riparian* issues like...

11. The greatest hits album attempts to *distill*...

Exercise II. Fill in the blank with the best word from the choices below. One word will not be used.

lavish	instill	riparian	lachrymal	ablution

1.   The Institute was dedicated to the study of _____ issues like erosion and streambed preservation.

2.   A(n) _____ array of features makes the new car perfect for the luxury buyer.

3.   Experience will _____ a healthy respect for nature into John.

4.   The patient with overactive _____ glands was always tearing up.

Fill in the blank with the best word from the choices below. One word will not be used.

meander	riparian	fluctuate	alluvial	distill

5.   The winemakers claim that their vintage will _____ the essence of a summer in Italy.

6.   Patrick watched the raindrops _____ down the windowpane, eventually making their way to the bottom.

7.   Water washing off the volcanic mountain changed the makeup of the _____ soil.

8.   Doctors were pleased that the patient's blood pressure did not _____, but remained steady.

Fill in the blank with the best word from the choices below. One word will not be used.

ablution	lachrymose	fluent	instill

9.   Reginald worried that no _____ would ever cleanse him of his sin.

10.   Laurie was a(n) _____ skier and often won first place in World Cup competitions.

11.   Donald feared that his best man, who was often sentimental, would make a(n) _____ speech at the wedding.

Exercise III. Choose the set of words that best completes the sentence.

1.   Diners _____ back and forth among the _____ tables, sampling the expensive foods.
      A.   lavished; distilled
      B.   meandered; lavish
      C.   instilled; riparian
      D.   distilled; fluent

2.   Although the author's writing is _____ and graceful, he focuses too much on _____ deathbed scenes and tearful breakups.
      A.   alluvial; lavish
      B.   lachrymose; riparian
      C.   fluent; lachrymose
      D.   meandering; lachrymal

3.   In the process of developing a _____ solution, the researchers had to _____ thousands of human tears.
      A.   fluent; instill
      B.   lachrymal; distill
      C.   riparian; distill
      D.   lavish; meander

4.   Some of the features of the _____ landscape include _____ formations deposited millions of years ago.
     A.   alluvial; lachrymal
     B.   lavish; lachrymose
     C.   riparian; alluvial
     D.   lachrymal; lavish

5.   Even if your teachers _____ the importance of good study habits into you, your grades may sometimes

     _____.
     A.   instill; fluctuate
     B.   meander; instill
     C.   distill; meander
     D.   fluctuate; distill

Exercise IV. Complete the sentence by inferring information about the italicized word from its context.

1.   A *lachrymose* television series will probably make its viewers…

2.   Looking at the *lavish* array of wedding gifts, the bride and groom may feel…

3.   If a doctor does not perform the required *ablution* before surgery, it is likely that…

Exercise V. Fill in each blank with the word from the Unit that best completes the sentence, using the root we supply as a clue. Then, answer the questions that follow the paragraphs.

Nothing can _____ (STILL) a fear of nature like a wall of water the size of a multi-story building. Such waves do come ashore every so often, especially in countries bordering the Pacific Ocean. The easiest place for them to strike is in harbors, where the elevation of the land is low, and so the Japanese word for the great rush of water, *tsunami*, literally means "harbor wave."

Most tsunamis begin on the ocean floor. Perhaps an undersea volcano erupts suddenly, or an earthquake with a magnitude of more than seven on the Richter Scale occurs along an ocean fault line. Whatever the cause, the land shifts suddenly.

What happens next is much like what happens when you bury your foot in ocean sand and then remove it quickly. The hole your foot makes does not remain a hole for long; water and sand fill it almost immediately. The same process—with billions of times more power behind it—is at work in a tsunami. Water rushes in to fill the vacancy left by the land.

The force of the water moving in pushes other water outward, and such displacement results in the tsunami that eventually affects human beings. Just as ripples flow out in concentric circles from the place where a stone drops into a lake, waves of energy in the form of displaced water move outward from the site of the undersea event. Unlike the ripples, though, these waves can grow to heights of sixty feet or more. And while a normal wave _____

(MEANDER) along at only a few miles per hour, a tsunami moves across the surface of the ocean at speeds that can reach five hundred miles an hour—faster than a jet plane.

The angle of the shore affects the force and turbulence of the incoming wave. A shoreline that gently slopes down toward the water will absorb energy more gradually than a steep incline or a cliff face. The shallow angle of many coastlines allows an incoming tsunami to advance a great distance before all its energy is expended. In fact, the monstrous tsunami of December 2004 released an amount of energy equal to 23,000 small nuclear bombs.

Few objects can withstand the onrush for long. Small wooden shacks, _____ (LAV) luxury hotels, heavy trains, cars, trees, boats, and people are swept away in the blink of an eye. The water quickly overruns any land that is lower than the edge of the shore. Farther away, the wave's intensity lessens, but even as far as three miles from the edge of the ocean, massive damage may be wreaked upon low-lying areas. The water then retreats, creating a false belief that the worst has passed.

Unfortunately, tsunamis are rarely composed of only one wave; usually, at least three strike the land. The largest number of deaths occurs after the first wave, when people who have survived walk outside to survey the damage and get caught by the next. This was the case in December 2004, when over two hundred thousand people lost their lives.

1. The author uses the example of a stone dropping into a lake to
    A. increase the reader's awareness of the power of water.
    B. introduce the thesis of the passage.
    C. give the reader an easily understood reference point.
    D. demonstrate a falling stone's potential force when dropped from a height.

2. The cause of a tsunami
    A. is not well understood.
    B. comes from the Japanese word for harbor wave.
    C. is not explained in the passage.
    D. is usually something that happens on the ocean floor.

3. What is the purpose of the final paragraph?
    A. It explains why tsunamis are often deadly to humans.
    B. It offers possible advice on preparation for tsunamis.
    C. It details the costs of a tsunami.
    D. It shows how little science actually knows about these disasters.

4. Judging by its use in the passage, the word *wreaked* probably means
    A. inflicted.
    B. ruined.
    C. scented.
    D. removed.

Exercise VI. Drawing on your knowledge of roots and words in context, read the following selection and define the italicized words. If you cannot figure out the meaning of the words on your own, look them up in a dictionary. Note that *ef* comes from *ex*, meaning "out."

Until the hospital windows were opened, the *effluvium* of death and disease wafted out into the hallways and settled over everything. A cool breeze was needed to *lave* the patients' bodies and minds. Bathed by the pleasant spring air, they recuperated much faster.

UNIT TWENTY-TWO

CREV
Latin CREPARE, CREPATUM, "to crack"

CREVICE (kre´ vəs) *n.* a small crack
Tony found the note tucked into a *crevice* in the wall.

CREVASSE (kre vas´) *n.* a large, deep crack; a chasm
We shouted frantically to the skier, who was heading in the direction of
the *crevasse*.
syn: *gap, cleft*

FISS
Latin FINDERE, FISSUS, "to split; to divide"

FISSION (fi´ shən) *n.* the splitting of something
Fission of the nucleus of uranium-235 generates several unstable subatomic
particles.

FISSURE (fi´ shər) *n.* an opening; a split
A *fissure* in the sea floor allowed superheated gases to escape upwards into
the ocean.

HIA
Latin HIARE, HISCENS, "to gape"

HIATUS (hī ā´ təs) *n.* an interruption in space or time; a gap
A brief *hiatus* in the discussion allowed the panelists to step outside for a
few moments.

The Latin crepatia *became the English* crevice *and* crevasse *through a very typical sound change. We can see another example of this in the Latin word* septa, *which became* seven *in English.*

The botanical suffix fid, *from* findere, *means "divided into parts or lobes." A* bifid *plant (*bi, *"two" +* fid*) may have a petal or leaf divided into two parts; a person with a* bifid *liver has a liver split into two parts.*

OS, OR
Latin OS, ORIS, "mouth; face"

OROTUND (or′ ə tənd) *adj.* 1. deep and full
2. pompous
L. *rotundus*, "round" + *oris* = *round-mouthed*
1. The speaker's *orotund* bass voice reverberated throughout the room.
2. Governor Reid's *orotund* speech made many in the audience roll their eyes.

ORIFICE (or′ ə fəs) *n.* a mouth or opening
L. *oris* + *facere*, "to make" = *mouth making*
The small birds stored their winter seeds in an *orifice* of the tree.

CAV
Latin CAVUS, "hollow"

EXCAVATE (ek′ skə vāt) *v.* to dig up
L. *ex*, "out" + *cavare* = *to hollow out*
Archaeologists have *excavated* an ancient Mayan village from a hillside beside a shopping mall.

CAVERNOUS (ka′ vərn əs) *adj.* deep and empty, like a cavern
Claudette hesitated before entering the *cavernous* bedchamber.

I was terrified to enter the CAVERNOUS CAVE.

CONCAVE (kän kāv′) *adj.* curving inward; hollowed
L. *com*, intensifier, + *cavus* = *hollowed out*
The space probe began sliding downward on the *concave* surface of the lakebed.

⚏ The Latin word for "little face" is oscilla. What English word is derived from oscilla?

⚏ When nuclear weapons were tested in the mid-20th century, they were exploded several hundred feet or more above the ground, under the ground, underwater, and in the atmosphere. Those that exploded underground created cavernous craters, sometimes hundreds of feet in diameter.

EXERCISES - UNIT TWENTY-TWO

Exercise I. Complete the sentence in a way that shows you understand the meaning of the italicized vocabulary word.

1. In order to *excavate* the dinosaur's skeleton, we…

2. The few scraggly plants that grew in the *crevice* must have been able to…

3. The *cavernous* airport hangar would have been a good place for…

4. There were a few unnecessary *orifices* in…

5. The gradual *fission* of the cell wall made…

6. Although the band said that they were taking a *hiatus* to work on solo projects,…

7. The potter turned the disc into a *concave* dish by…

8. Lowering herself into the *crevasse*, Simone found…

9. When the hot gases reached the *fissure* in the volcano, they…

10. When I heard the singer's *orotund* voice, I pictured him as…

Exercise II. Fill in the blank with the best word from the choices below. One word will not be used.

cavernous   hiatus   concave   orifice

1. Where the huge building had once stood, there was now a(n) _____ space.

2. A(n) _____ on the whale's head allowed it to breathe.

3. After a yearlong _____, the senator returned to office.

Fill in the blank with the best word from the choices below. One word will not be used.

fissure   orotund   excavate   hiatus

4. An attempt to _____ the buried treasure will be dangerous because it is far underwater.

5. When we saw that the scheduled speaker was a famously _____ politician, we all took the afternoon off.

6. The _____ that ran from head to toe of my spacesuit had been caused by the sudden increase in pressure.

Fill in the blank with the best word from the choices below. One word will not be used.

crevasse   fission   excavate   crevice   concave

7.   The tiny bird took shelter in a(n) _____ in the wall.

8.   _____ of the atom resulted in the release of nuclear energy.

9.   Ice samples taken from deep within the _____ can give us clues about the planet during the first Ice Age.

10. Because the surface of the roller rink was _____, skaters tended to roll toward the center.

Exercise III. Choose the set of words that best completes the sentence.

1.   The earthquake turned a small _____ into a giant _____.
     A.   crevice; hiatus
     B.   fissure; crevasse
     C.   hiatus; fissure
     D.   crevasse; orifice

2.   The singer's famously _____ voice packed the _____ auditorium.
     A.   orotund; cavernous
     B.   orifice; concave
     C.   concave; orotund
     D.   cavernous; orotund

3.   The unusual _____ of the trunk as the tree grew resulted in a(n) _____ about an inch wide.
     A.   fission; hiatus
     B.   crevice; hiatus
     C.   fission; crevice
     D.   hiatus; orifice

4.   A(n) _____ in the winter storm allowed the builders to _____ the lumber that had been buried in snow.
     A.   fissure; excavate
     B.   orifice; fission
     C.   hiatus; concave
     D.   hiatus; excavate

5.   The _____ surface of the plant's leaves and the thousands of tiny _____ on each leaf helps the plant catch and absorb water.
     A.   cavernous; fissions
     B.   concave; orifices
     C.   orotund; hiatuses
     D.   concave; crevasses

Exercise IV. Complete the sentence by inferring information about the italicized word from its context.

1.   When Terrell hears the preacher's *orotund* sermon, he will probably...

2.   Students who volunteer to help *excavate* the ancient village will need tools like...

3.   During a *hiatus* in the thunderstorm, the children will probably...

Exercise V. Fill in each blank with the word from the Unit that best completes the sentence, using the root we supply as a clue. Then, answer the questions that follow the paragraphs.

Imagine that you live on the edge of a _____ (FISS) in the sea floor, thousands of feet below the ocean's surface. Superheated gases escape from the vent and rush upwards into the ocean. Your surroundings are far beyond the reach of the sun's rays, so your eyes do you no good. You're constantly either freezing or nearly boiled alive. And the mass of water pushing down on you means that every square inch of your body is under tremendous pressure. It would be astonishing if you survived, and yet life forms have adapted to the intense temperatures, pressure, and darkness of deep-ocean vent environments.

The most amazing-looking adaptations have come about as a result of the total darkness at the bottom of the sea. No sunlight penetrates the water at these depths, so photosynthesis, the process through which plants process sunlight to make food, is impossible. Plants are the foundation of the food chain, the energy source that allows all other life to continue. So how does anything grow this far underwater? Instead of depending on oxygen, the plant-like organisms at the bottom of the sea are *chemosynthetic*; they have evolved ways of using the minerals and heat emitted from the vents in the earth to fuel their own metabolisms. With such food available, larger creatures can also hang out in the dark. Some of them even take advantage of it. The anglerfish, for example, has a tiny, phosphorescent lure dangling from the inside of its mouth. When other creatures, attracted by the "light," come near, they are drawn into the fish's _____ (OR) and devoured.

But although plants and animals have come up with their own food sources in the absence of sunlight, they cannot replace the sun's heat. The temperature of the water stays around 35 degrees Fahrenheit—too cold for many animals to survive. Again, adaptation comes into play: the vents are home to creatures that have evolved to endure, and even thrive in, near-freezing temperatures. They have extra portions of certain fatty acids, as well as special proteins that keep the water within their cells from freezing.

While the water at the bottom of the deep ocean is very cold, the temperatures of the chimney vents can reach above 700 degrees Fahrenheit. Some tubeworms living on the edge of thermal vents may be subjected to differences in temperature of as much as 50 degrees between their bases and tips. These animals must be able to withstand not just one extreme temperature, but the whole vast range of hot and cold between superheated gases and icy-cold waters.

And they must overcome an obstacle we might not even think about: the weight of the water itself. Up to 15,000 pounds of pressure press down on every square inch. To meet this challenge, many of the deep-sea-vent organisms have become barophiles (from the Greek *baros*, "weight")— creatures that thrive in high-pressure environments. They have adapted to conditions that would kill anything living in a lower-pressure environment by evolving bodies without any air spaces. Their cell membranes also contain greater amounts of certain substances that help them stay flexible.

An environment so different from that of our own that it could be on another planet exists at the bottom of the sea. Ironically, the differences in respiration, cell structure, and energy absorption can help us better understand our own bodies and the way we interact with our surroundings.

1.   From the passage, we can guess that metabolism is associated with
   A. cooperation.
   B. adaptation.
   C. energy.
   D. temperature.

2.   Judging by the sixth paragraph, the author is about to discuss
      A. uses of deep-sea research for human biology.
      B. chemosynthetic adaptations of marine organisms.
      C. the effect of high pressure on humans.
      D. similarities between the land and ocean environments.

3.   Because chemosynthesis is possible around the deep-ocean vents,
      A. oxygen does not go to waste underwater.
      B. lack of sunlight does not prevent mineral absorption.
      C. life around the vents is not destroyed by heat.
      D. organisms like the anglerfish are able to survive.

4.   In the introduction, the author emphasizes
      A. the harsh conditions around the vents.
      B. the adaptation of organisms to cold.
      C. the primary role of sunlight in ocean environments.
      D. the importance of adaptation.

5.   The author of the passage probably believes that
      A. survival in extreme conditions is likely, but not proven.
      B. organisms change to meet the challenges of their environments.
      C. human beings are unable to adapt to extreme conditions.
      D. all organisms benefit from the challenges of their environments.

Exercise VI. Drawing on your knowledge of roots and words in context, read the following selection and define the italicized words. If you cannot figure out the meaning of the words on your own, look them up in a dictionary.

Because our designated *ostiary* couldn't make it, Gene stood by the church door to welcome visitors and hand out programs for the service. He also entertained the guests with stories of the church's early days and facts about its construction. Few of them knew that an especially *fissile* stone had been chosen so that the church bricks could be easily and quickly cut.

VOCABULARY WORD LIST FOR BOOKS IN THIS SERIES

Level VII
abbreviate
abduct
absolute
accessible
accompaniment
adjacent
aerate
aerial
affection
affirmative
agenda
airy
alleviate
ambition
analogy
apologetic
appendix
application
apprehend
ascertain
asocial
aspire
associate
assumption
attentive
attractive
ballistic
biographical
brevity
brutality
brute
capacity
capitalize
captivate
celebrant
celebratory
celebrity
certainty
certify
circumstance
coagulate
companionship
complex
composition
comprehend
compute
concerted
condense
conduct
confidante
confident
confirm
conscience
conservative
constant
constrict
consume
contract
convection
convict
cooperate
course
creed
currency
decapitate
deficient
deflate
defunct

deliverance
delude
denounce
density
deposit
descriptive
diagram
discount
discredit
disintegrate
dismantle
dispense
distract
domestic
domicile
dominate
dominion
duplicate
effortless
elevate
elongate
emaciated
emancipate
encompass
evaluate
evict
exhilarating
expire
fabled
fabulous
facsimile
fortify
fortitude
frugal
fruitful
gradual
grave
gravity
hilarity
host
hostile
hyperventilate
ideal
idealistic
idealize
illogical
illusion
impermanent
impress
incredible
infirm
inflate
inoperable
integrate
integrity
intend
invalid
invaluable
jubilant
jubilee
leverage
levitate
liberal
liberate
linguistic
literal
literate
malfunction
mantled

manual
manufacture
manuscript
meager
militant
militarize
multilingual
mythical
mythology
narrate
narrative
obliterate
observant
occurrence
omnipotent
operational
opponent
oppress
oral
oration
oratory
parable
passable
petrify
possessive
potent
preservation
presumptuous
procession
produce
program
progression
projectile
prolong
pronounce
proposition
prosecute
rapidity
rapture
recipient
recount
recurrent
regal
regicide
reign
remnant
reputation
restriction
reveal
savor
savvy
scientific
sensation
sensible
sentimental
sequel
sequence
sociable
socialize
solution
spirited
stationary
status
subject
subscribe
succession
suffice
sumptuous
suspend

symbolize
textile
texture
transact
transgress
transit
unveil
validate
vehicle
ventilate
victorious

Level VIII
abhor
abundant
accelerated
administer
admission
advisable
agile
agitate
allege
amnesty
anarchy
annals
annual
annuity
antediluvian
anticipate
appreciative
arbiter
arbitrary
arbitrate
archaic
arid
aspersion
assiduous
astronomical
autonomous
avail
castigate
cataclysmic
celestial
censor
censure
chastened
chastise
chronic
chronology
cloister
cohabitation
commensurate
composure
conceive
condone
confines
connoisseur
consolidate
conspicuous
contemporaneous
contemporary
corroborate
deceptive
deify
deign
deity
deluge
demented
demote

depreciate
derivative
desist
despicable
deter
detract
diagnosis
differentiate
dilute
dimension
disclose
discourse
disdain
disperse
dissident
donor
durable
duration
editorial
emergent
enact
enduring
energetic
enumerate
ergonomic
evident
exaggerated
exceptional
excursion
exhibit
exhume
exponential
extol
extract
finite
formidable
forte
fortitude
founder
frequent
fugitive
fundamental
fusion
horrific
humility
hypothesis
idiom
idiosyncrasy
immense
immerse
immovable
imposition
impunity
inconstant
indeterminate
indignant
infrequent
ingest
innumerable
inoculate
insidious
instantaneous
insular
insulate
inter
intercept
interminable
intersperse
intimidate

intrepid
intuitive
inveterate
invigorate
irreverent
jurisdiction
jurisprudence
litigant
litigation
magisterial
magistrate
matriarch
mentality
minister
mnemonic
mobile
monotheism
nebulous
nemesis
nimbus
nonplussed
nontraditional
notorious
ocular
omission
pantheon
parenthetical
participant
perjure
persistent
plurality
polytheistic
preliminary
preside
prodigal
prognosis
punitive
ration
rational
reactionary
reconnaissance
redundant
reference
refine
refuge
refuse
reinstate
repository
residual
respective
revere
revise
rivulet
robust
sanctify
sanctions
sanctuary
sanctum
seclude
sedentary
single
singular
solidarity
sparse
stellar
subliminal
submerge
submissive
subpoena

subsidiary
subsist
subterfuge
subterranean
suggestible
supersede
surgical
surplus
suspect
syndicate
synthesize
tempo
terminal
terrestrial
terrorize
timorous
torrent
torrid
trepidation
tutelage
unrivaled
valiant
valor
veteran
vigorous
vista
volatile

Level IX
abjure
abstain
accord
adept
affable
affiliate
affluent
agenda
alias
alienate
allegation
alleviate
alteration
altercation
alternate
amble
ambulatory
amiable
amicable
analogous
animosity
anonymous
antagonist
antagonize
antebellum
antibiotic
antonym
aptitude
aristocracy
assonance
audit
auditory
bellicose
belligerence
benefactor
benevolent
benign
bibliophile
biodegradable
bureaucrat

138

cadence
casualty
cede
circumspect
cognitive
cognizant
collapse
concession
confound
conjure
consecutive
cordial
corporeal
corpulent
courier
decadent
delegate
denomination
deplete
dialogue
dictum
digress
dilate
diminish
discord
disenchanted
dismal
dispel
disposition
dissemble
dissonance
divest
domineering
edict
effigy
elapse
elucidate
enamored
enjoin
enunciate
equanimity
equilibrium
equitable
exacting
execution
expatriate
expedient
figment
filial
formative
genealogy
gradualism
herbivorous
homogenized
homonym
immortalize
impart
impartial
impediment
implement
impose
improvise
inalienable
inaudible
incantation
incision
inclusive
incognito
inconclusive

inconsequential
incorporate
incur
indecisive
indict
indomitable
ineffable
inept
infantile
infuse
inhibit
iniquity
injunction
invidious
invoke
leaven
legacy
legislative
legitimize
levity
lucid
magnanimous
magnate
magnitude
malevolent
malicious
maternal
matriculate
matron
maxim
megalomaniac
megalopolis
mellifluous
metabolism
metamorphosis
metaphorical
microcosm
microscopic
miniscule
minute
misinformation
monogamy
monolithic
monologue
monopolize
morbid
moribund
mortify
nomenclature
nominal
noxious
omnivorous
partisan
paternal
patricide
patronize
pedagogue
pedant
pedestrian
perceptible
perjury
pernicious
philanthropy
philosophical
phosphorescent
photogenic
phototropic
posit
preamble

precept
precise
preclude
predominant
prefigure
privileged
proactive
progenitor
progeny
prohibit
prologue
pronouncement
propel
prospect
protagonist
providential
provocative
rapacious
rapt
recant
recede
recurrent
reform
regress
rejoinder
relapse
relative
renounce
replete
repulsion
resonant
retinue
revival
revoke
semblance
simulate
sophisticate
sophistry
sophomoric
specter
suffuse
superfluous
superlative
surreptitious
susceptible
sustain
symbiotic
synonymous
tenacious
theocracy
translucent
travesty
unanimous
uniform
unison
vested
vestment
vivacious
vivid
voracious

Level X
aberrant
abject
abrogate
acerbic
acquisitive
acrid
acrimonious

adherent
admonition
adverse
advocate
aesthetic
anatomy
anesthetic
annotate
antipathy
apathetic
apolitical
apparition
approbation
arrogant
aspect
avarice
avid
benediction
bibulous
cautionary
cautious
circumvent
civic
civility
civilize
clamorous
colloquial
compel
complacent
comportment
compunction
conciliatory
concise
conducive
confer
confide
congress
conjecture
connotation
conscientious
constructive
construe
convene
convoluted
correspond
cosmopolitan
counsel
covenant
credence
credible
credulity
crucial
crux
culpable
culprit
cursory
declaim
decriminalize
deduce
defer
deference
definitive
deflect
degrade
dejected
demagogue
demographic
denotation
deprecate

derogatory
despondent
destitute
deviate
diaphanous
dichotomy
dictate
diffident
diffuse
diligent
dismissive
dispute
disreputable
dissolute
dissuade
docile
doctrine
doleful
dolorous
dubious
effervescent
effusive
egress
eloquent
emissary
emote
empathy
envisage
epiphany
epitome
equivocate
errant
erroneous
espouse
evince
evocative
evolve
exacerbate
excise
exclamatory
excruciating
exonerate
expel
expound
extort
facile
facsimile
factotum
fallacious
fallacy
fallible
fervent
fervor
fetid
fidelity
fractious
glut
glutton
gratuitous
gustatory
gusto
imbibe
impervious
impetuous
impetus
imprecation
impulse
impute
incisive

incoherent
incredulous
incriminate
incursion
indoctrinate
indolent
indubitable
induce
inference
infinite
infinitesimal
inflection
inflexible
infraction
infrastructure
infringe
ingrate
ingratiate
inherent
innovative
inquisitive
insipid
insoluble
intact
intemperate
interrogate
intractable
introspective
invincible
irrational
locution
malediction
malodorous
mea culpa
motif
motive
novel
novice
obviate
odoriferous
olfactory
onerous
onus
palatable
palate
pandemic
pathos
penultimate
perspicacious
persuasion
petulant
phenomenon
placebo
placid
politicize
precarious
precaution
precursor
premonition
prescient
presentiment
primacy
primal
primeval
proffer
proficient
profuse
proliferate
proponent

protracted
provincial
punctilious
pungent
purported
putrefy
putrid
rancid
rancor
rationale
rationalize
recollect
reconcile
recourse
recrimination
redolent
redoubtable
remiss
reprobate
reprove
requisition
resolute
restitution
retort
retract
retrospective
revert
sacrilege
sapient
sentient
sentiment
sentinel
stagnant
stagnate
stature
subvert
sycophant
tactile
tangible
temper
temperance
tome
tortuous
ultimate
ultimatum
unconscionable
viaduct
virile
virtue
virtuoso
visage
voluble

Level XI
ablution
abominable
abomination
accede
acclivity
acquiesce
adorn
adventitious
alluvial
ambiance
annex
antecedent
appall
append
appraise

appreciable
apropos
ascertain
assertion
attrition
auspices
auspicious
bacchanal
bacchic
belabor
candid
candor
catholic
cavernous
certitude
circuitous
communal
concave
conferment
conflagration
congested
consort
consortium
consummate
contort
contravene
contrite
converge
crevasse
crevice
declivity
decorous
decorum
demerit
demonstrative
denigrate
depose
deracinate
desolate
destine
desultory
detrimental
detritus
discomfit
disconcert
disseminate
dissertation
distill
distort
diverge
divulge
ecstasy
edification
elaborate
elegiac
elegy
entity
eradicate
essence
euphoria
excavate
excommunicate
exertion
expendable
extant
exultant
feasible
festoon

fete
fission
fissure
flagrant
flamboyant
florid
flourish
fluctuate
fluent
formality
formulaic
formulate
fortuitous
fortuity
fulminate
germane
germinal
germinate
gestate
gesticulate
hiatus
hoi polloi
holistic
illustrative
illustrious
impair
impeccable
impending
implicit
importunate
importune
incandescent
incendiary
incense
incommunicado
inexplicable
inflammatory
inordinate
insinuate
instill
insufferable
interject
inundate
irradicable
jocose
jocular
laborious
lachrymal
lachrymose
languid
languish
languor
lavish
lenient
lenitive
lethargy
liaison
ligature
liturgy
livid
luster
magnum opus
malaise
malfeasance
malign
malinger
meander
meretricious

meritorious
metaphrase
modus operandi
mollify
monosyllabic
monotone
monotonous
munificent
negate
negligent
negligible
nexus
obligatory
ominous
opulent
ordain
orifice
ornate
orotund
pallid
pallor
paradigm
paraphrase
parcel
parse
parvenu
peccadillo
peccant
pejorative
periphery
phraseology
plaint
plaintive
polyglot
polymath
precedent
predestination
preferential
preordained
proclivity
propitiate
propitious
quintessential
quittance
rapport
redound
refulgent
remonstrate
remunerate
repartee
requiem
resilient
restive
riparian
rudiment
rudimentary
sedition
semantic
seminal
semiotic
sinuous
soliloquy
solipsism
somnolent
sopor
soporific
stanch
stasis

static
staunch
subjective
suborn
summation
surfeit
synergy
totalitarian
totality
transitory
trenchant
trite
truncate
undulate
verdant
verdure
vigilant
vigilante
viridity
vulgar

Level XII
abscond
abstruse
adduce
adjourn
adjudicate
adroit
adumbrate
aggregate
agrarian
alacrity
allocate
allude
amoral
anachronism
anathema
animadversion
aperture
apocryphal
apposite
apprise
artifice
artless
ascribe
aspire
assay
asset
attenuate
avocation
bucolic
capitulate
caprice
celerity
chronicle
circumlocution
circumscribe
cogent
cognate
colloquy
collusion
complicity
composite
comprise
concede
concordance
concur
confluence

conjugal
consecrate
consign
conspire
constrain
contend
context
contiguous
contingent
covert
cryptic
defray
degenerate
demise
demur
demure
derisive
devoid
diabolical
discern
discordant
discrete
discretion
discursive
distend
diurnal
dour
duplicitous
duress
dystopian
egregious
emblematic
emulate
engender
ensue
episodic
epithet
esprit
evanescent
execrable
exigent
expiate
explicate
extemporaneous
extenuating
feign
felicitous
felicity
fictive
flux
fruition
fruitless
genre
gregarious
hyperbole
icon
iconoclast
iconography
idyllic
impious
implicate
in lieu of
inanimate
incessant
incite
inconsolable
incorrigible
incurious

inert
inexplicable
infelicitous
influx
infrangible
inimitable
innate
innocuous
insatiable
insuperable
intercede
interlude
internecine
interpose
intransigent
intrusive
inveigh
irrepressible
judicious
locus
loquacious
ludicrous
magniloquent
methodical
moratorium
mores
morose
myopic
nascent
obdurate
obloquy
obsequious
obtrusive
ostensible
overt
parturient
pastoral
peregrination
perpetuate
perpetuity
pertinacious
perturb
plenary
plenipotentiary
portend
precipitate
prestige
pretext
procure
proscribe
proviso
psyche
psychosomatic
psychotic
purveyor
purview
pusillanimous
recapitulate
recondite
rectify
rectitude
refract
remit
repast
repertory
reprehensible
reprimand
reserved

resignation
resuscitate
reticent
risible
rustic
sacrosanct
salubrious
salutary
salutation
satiety
sectarian
segue
servile
signatory
sinecure
sojourn
solace
solicitous
sovereign
stricture
stringent
subdue
subjugate
subservient
subtext
succor
suffrage
suppress
surfeit
surmise
synchronous
synod
synopsis
tacit
taciturn
temporal
temporize
tenable
tendentious
tenet
tenuous
topical
traduce
transect
transfigure
transpire
turbid
turbulent
umbrage
univocal
utopian
vacuity
vacuous
vaunted
vehement
verbatim
verbiage
verbose
vocation
vociferous